MAURIAC
the politics of a novelist

MAURIAC
the politics of a novelist

MALCOLM SCOTT

1980

SCOTTISH ACADEMIC PRESS
EDINBURGH

Published by
Scottish Academic Press Ltd,
33 Montgomery Street
Edinburgh EH7 5JX

ISBN 7073 0262 5

Printed in Great Britain
by Clark Constable Ltd, Edinburgh

CONTENTS

ACKNOWLEDGEMENTS

As this book grew out of one small section of a doctoral thesis on Mauriac's work, I should like to take this opportunity of thanking my supervisor, Mrs Annie Barnes, for her kind encouragement during that early period of my research. I express my thanks also to others who have read and commented on this book at various stages of its development, and especially to Professor Richard Griffiths and Dr John Coombes. The many remaining weaknesses are of course my own responsibility.

I am indebted to the Carnegie Trust and to the Publications and Muniments Committee of the University of St. Andrews for their generous assistance towards publication costs, and to the Court of the University of St. Andrews for helping to finance research in France.

I am grateful also to M. François Chapon, director of the Bibliothèque Littéraire Jacques Doucet, for providing access to manuscript material in the Fonds Mauriac, and to the Editorial Committee of *Forum for Modern Language Studies* for permission to include, in modified form, material first published in that journal in April 1971 (in an article entitled 'The Sillon and Mauriac's first published writings').

I record also my profound gratitude to François Mauriac for his interest in my research and for his hospitality during a visit which I made to Malagar.

PREFACE

As a subject for a book, Mauriac's politics may appear, especially to a British reader, to belong to the same category as Ingres' violin. Mauriac was not a politician. He was never in a position from which he could directly control or shape the events of his life-time. Nor even, at any stage, was he a member of a political party.[1] He was a major novelist who, around the age of fifty, began a second career as a political commentator and became, beyond all expectation, one of the most widely read and controversial political journalists of the next three decades. His writings on politics were mostly in the form of articles, written regularly over a period of more than thirty years for a succession of papers and magazines—notably *L'Écho de Paris*, *Le Figaro* and *Le Figaro littéraire*, *Le Temps présent*, *La Table ronde* and *L'Express*. Most of these articles have been collected in book form in his *Journal* (particularly volumes Four and Five), in *Le Bâillon dénoué*, in *Mémoires politiques* and in the five volumes of *Bloc-notes*. In addition, there was his wartime book *Le Cahier noir* and, towards the end of his life, his *De Gaulle*. He also contributed prefaces to various political works, some of which can be consulted in the anthology *D'Autres et moi*. This book is a study of the political and social outlook expressed in this large body of writing and of its relationship to the period through which Mauriac lived. It also considers what might be called the pre-history of Mauriac's political thought, examining the essays, literary articles and, where relevant, novels which, although written before his entry into the arena of journalism, reflect aspects of their author's temperament which help to throw light on his later political options.

No previous study has been made of the totality of these writings. A handful of writers, compared to the much larger number of those who have written about Mauriac the novelist, have commented on his political attitudes, but most of these have approached their subject with an all too visible political axe to grind, and in such a hostile or caricatural spirit as to invalidate their essays as serious accounts of his politics. This applies, it seems to me, to the books by Pol Vandromme and Jacques Laurent, as well as to Maurice Bardèche's *Lettre ouverte*.[2] Xavier Grall's *Mauriac journaliste*[3] gives due credit to some of Mauriac's more courageous stands, but is marred by a self-confessed emotional reaction to the events described. It is also strictly limited in scope and was published at a time when Mauriac had ten more years ahead of him in which to observe and comment on the French and world scene. Jean de Fabrègues' chapter 'Mauriac politique', in his recent general study[4], gives a more complete view. Written as it is by a man who knew Mauriac well and who is a prolific writer on 'Catholic politics', it clearly commands attention. It too is limited, however, both in length and ambition, drawing almost exclusively from the articles selected by Mauriac for inclusion in the *Mémoires politiques* and from the few politically relevant sections of the *Mémoires intérieurs*. Another recent general book on Mauriac, Robert Speaight's biography[5], offers a reliable narrative account of Mauriac's political involvement without much concern for political ideas.

The gap exists, therefore, in Mauriac studies, and this book is written in the conviction that it is worth filling. Mauriac was a figure of such stature in modern French intellectual and literary life that an understanding of an area of his work which dominated the second half of his career as a writer is necessary to complete our view of him. Furthermore, a claim can be made for the recognition of Mauriac as an important exponent of French nationalist writing. In making this claim, this book explores his relationship to men like Barrès, Maurras and de Gaulle and seeks to throw some light on French nationalist literature in general.

This study does not set out to be a comprehensive narrative of Mauriac's political activities or friendships. Such an account will not be possible before the release of personal papers belonging to Mauriac and others. Apart from a small number of instances in which I have succumbed to the temptation of factual narrative—because of the special interest of the events concerned, or to correct errors in other accounts or support my argument relating to Mauriac's standpoint at various times in his career—this is a study of attitudes and ideas underlying Mauriac's public activity and statements of position. I have allowed myself, in pursuit of an understanding of the relationship of these attitudes and ideas to Mauriac's work as a creative writer and to his religious faith, to include material and follow paths that might have been eschewed in a narrower interpretation of Mauriac's politics. This is especially so in Chapter Two, which is a study of the constant interweaving of literary, moral and religious issues with political ones in Mauriac's work.

Part One

TOWARDS A POLITICAL
TEMPERAMENT

Chapter One

FIRST ENCOUNTERS

(i) *Introduction: constants and options*

The Marist fathers have run their residence for Catholic students at 104 rue de Vaugirard, Paris, for several generations. It is called the Réunion des Étudiants, and it was there, on February 12th, 1908, that a discusson group known as the Conférence Saint-Paul listened to a lecture given by one of their number who was destined to become (François Mitterrand not withstanding) the Réunion's most celebrated former resident. The speaker was François Mauriac, then twenty-two years old, and his subject—a topical one in those days of *revanchard* patriotism—was 'L'Idée de Patrie'. The lecture is of interest not only because it was the first expression by Mauriac of his views on a political subject, but also because it already reflected, three decades before his emergence as a recognised political commentator, the pre-occupations of his later life.[1] He urged upon his fellow students, as he would urge on the readers of his political column, the importance of patriotic sentiment. Patriotism was a noble and disinterested emotion, he told them. More, indeed, than an emotion, it was an instinct, implanted in Frenchmen by their forefathers, a part of their individual and collective birth-right. But, he warned, there were dangers of excess. Mother France stood high in the scale of eternal values, but not so high as God or Justice. Certain nationalists were in peril of forgetting this, and should remember the words of Lacordaire: 'Celui qui emploie des moyens misérables, même pour sauver son pays, celui-là demeure toujours un misérable.' Furthermore, patriotism was not the prerogative of the political Right, with which in recent years it had become seemingly irrevocably associated. To illustrate this, Mauriac quoted approvingly from a speech of Jean Jaurès on the patriotic fervour of the French workman, and reminded his audience

3

that, as an historic teacher of Liberty, France's mission in the world was a democratic one—a refutation of the view, often expressed at that time, that democrats and patriots were of two mutually alien species.

In this brief summary of an early and no doubt immature lecture, certain constants of Mauriac's political outlook can be traced, each of which can be ascribed to influences acting upon him in the early years of his life. His deep pride at being a Frenchman is one of these constants, and when, as in his lecture, he bases it upon respect for the memory of 'les générations disparues' and 'la foule immense des morts', he reminds his reader at once of his frequently avowed debt to the nationalist writer Maurice Barrès. A second constant lies in a certain coldness towards other exponents of nationalism, despite a fascination with some of their ideas. When he accuses them of short-comings on the moral and religious planes, he is clearly alluding, without needing to mention them by name, to Charles Maurras and the men of the Action Française. A third constant, arising partly out of the second, is his determination to avoid following the mainstream of nationalist opinion into the excesses of anti-democratic prejudice; and here, perhaps, his debt is to Marc Sangnier's Christian social movement, Le Sillon, of which he was a member for a short time around the age of twenty. And finally, over-riding yet uniting all of these leitmotifs in his political thought, there was his lifelong adherence to the Christian faith and to the Catholic Church. God was not to cede first place, he said in his lecture, not even to the fatherland. True patriotism did not seek to promote itself above Christian duty, but blended with it, and incorporated also the fraternal spirit of democracy, so that the essential goal was to 'préparer une France plus chrétienne et plus fraternelle'.

Catholicism, patriotism, the lesson of the Sillon, a mixture of attraction and opposition to the doctrines of Maurras: these are the ingredients of Mauriac's political creed. There are several different versions of how they were inter-related, most of them provided by Mauriac himself. He was torn between the desire to project an image of consistency (like most men involved in politics or political com-mentary) and the urge, an artist's urge, to dramatise the conflicting strands in his outlook; and this results in his viewing the foundations of his beliefs from somewhat different angles according to the circum-stances in which his declarations of faith were made. At times we find him insisting on an undeviating line of development on the liberal or even 'left' margin of Catholic opinion from his Sillonist days to the time of the Mouvement Républicain Populaire and beyond. Writing of Marc Sangnier in 1951, he declared: 'Je ne lui suis resté fidèle que quelques mois, mais ils ont suffi: j'avais compris pour toujours.'[2] And when, in the 1960s, his fervent support of de Gaulle saw him categorised as a man of the Right who had forgotten his earlier professions of belief in democracy, he harked back indefatigably to what he liked to see (and liked others to see) as the left-wing influence of his contact with the Sillon, which he once described as the thread that had led him through the maze of French politics.[3] Correspondingly, he claimed more than once to be a lifelong adversary of the movement which opposed the liberal Sillon, namely the nationalist and monarchist Action Française. In his book on de Gaulle and elsewhere he insists on an unswerving opposition to Maurras' integral nationalism.[4]

Polemical necessity played some part in the categorical nature of these statements. Between the Liberation and the mid-1960s, it was manifestly prudent of Mauriac to dissociate himself totally from Maurras and from the movement which stood discredited, as did many of its Catholic supporters, after its involvement in the tragic history of Vichy. But towards the end of his life, the situation had changed. Mauriac had a growing sense of invulnerability to criticism, stemming both from his awareness of approaching death, which placed political dispute in perspective, and from his certainty, until the traumatic spring and summer of 1968, of having ended up for once on the winning side in politics. Thus he felt able to present his private political history in a more interesting dialectical light. In the preface to the *Mémoires politiques*, published in 1967, he admitted a basic contradiction in his views. There was the Sillon's ineradicable influence, certainly; but on the other hand there were factors which drew him instinctively to the Right, not least the middle-class, mercantile and Catholic environment into which he was born. There was also his admiration for Barrès (and, he says in *De Gaulle*, for the nationalist historian Jacques Bainville[5]) and his interest in Maurras, of whose newspaper he became a daily reader though a critical one. These writers helped to instil in him what he calls, using de Gaulle's famous phrase, 'une certaine idée de la France'.[6] And only in what he terms 'the Gaullist dialectic' did he eventually harmonise these leanings to both Left and Right.[7]

The vantage points have thus already been plotted from which to survey Mauriac's progress from his early membership of the Sillon through the apparently uncommitted period of the 1920s and early 1930s and up to his intervention as a fledgling polemicist into the ideological battles that were waged in France after Mussolini's invasion of Ethiopia and the outbreak of war in Spain; and from there through the years of Occupation and Resistance to the Liberation, through the frustrating years (for him) of the Fourth Republic to the return to power of his ultimate master de Gaulle. His ideas underwent a marked development during these many years, but they had their roots in the encounters of his youth, in his reading of Barrès and Maurras, in his association with Sangnier's movement, in the wealthy bourgeois home into which he was born and in the Catholic faith that was his from childhood. That early period of his life is the starting-point for this study.

(ii) *Bordeaux, Barrès and the Sillon*

The political choices facing Mauriac as a young man were determined firstly by his situation as a Catholic in Third Republican France. The writer whose work, in all of its many aspects, was to be indissolubly linked with his Catholic faith was born in 1885, at a time when the prestige of the Church in France was at a low ebb and when quarrels raged amongst Catholics themselves. The closing decades of the nineteenth century and the first few years of the twentieth constituted one of the most critical periods in the history of the French Church, due to the seemingly irrevocable decline in Church–State relations. Catholics were identified as supporters of the various adversaries against which the recently instituted Third Republic had had to establish itself, and were now a target in their turn of the confident and consolidated Republican regime. Behind these recent points of dispute lay more ancient hatreds between Catholics and Republicans. In the eyes of radical Republicans the Church was a pillar of outmoded authority that, by mischance or mismanagement, had been left standing among the ruins of the *Ancien Régime*. It was seen as cherishing conceptions of social organisation that were alien to the modern age and, regardless of its official policy of neutrality towards any particular type of political system, it appeared in practice to prefer regimes which all but the most authoritarian Republican found excessively conservative. It had been allowed to redress itself by the Concordat and to re-establish its power during the monarchical and imperial interludes of the nineteenth century, but now the work of the Revolution had to be completed. The Church must be dispossessed of its ability to shape the minds of present and future Frenchmen. The Catholics, for their part, saw themselves beleaguered by a radical Republicanism which many of them did not distinguish from the terrifying face of the Revolution itself. Albert de Mun spoke for many of his co-religionaries when he wrote: 'Entre l'Église et la Révolution, il y a incompatibilité; il faut que l'Église tue la Révolution ou bien que la Révolution tue l'Église.'[8] Through the 1880s the second of these alternatives seemed by far the more likely, as the secularisation of France's laws and institutions got under way. The 1890s saw an unexpected lull in the conflict, due both to the Méline government's attempt to create an 'esprit nouveau' in the interests of national unity and to Pope Leo XIII's launching of the Ralliement movement, aimed at encouraging Catholics to accept the existence of the Republic as a fact, however unpalatable, of political life. The situation was irrevocably aggravated, however, by the Dreyfus Affair, dividing Catholics and liberal Republicans into two violently opposed camps. The impossibly bad relations thus created paved the way for the fiercely anti-clerical measures of the early years of the new century and, eventually, for the Separation of Church and State in 1905.

The old myth, according to which a man could not easily be both a Catholic and a Republican, seemed confirmed; and it held very fast in the milieu into which Mauriac was born. His native city of Bordeaux had strong royalist traditions, having been the first of France's large towns to open its gates to the monarchy at the end of Napoleon's reign.[9] During Mauriac's youth, antipathy to the Republic was especially strong there, above all in the great wine-producing families, closely linked to Britain by traditional commercial ties and envying the relative stability, so propitious to commerce, which they saw in this country from across the sea. Mauriac's own family, whose fortune had been made in timber and which stood somewhat lower in Bordeaux's finely graduated social scale, nevertheless shared the same conservative conception of society, seeing no offence to man or God in the thrifty accumulation of capital.[10] They held in deep suspicion, as dire threats to their material comfort, the economic outlook of the Republican Left. Yet this very family was split, like the nation as a whole, over the religious question; a split with political as well as philosophical implications. To the stern Catholicism of Mauriac's mother's family, the Coiffards, the paternal line opposed its anticlericalism. Mauriac's grandfather, before the eleventh-hour con-

version often related by Mauriac, was a resolute enemy of the local
Marist fathers. His son Jean-Paul Mauriac, the novelist's father,
proudly signed a letter, during his military service, 'soldat de la
République';[11] while his brother, Mauriac's uncle Louis, had been in
his youth something of a political *enfant terrible*, a reputation he was
to enhance by his support for Dreyfus in later years. Yielding to his
occasional desire to dramatise his ideological and temperamental
heritage, Mauriac later presented these differences between the Coiffards and the Mauriacs as being at the root of his own contradictions.[12]
In truth, his father's untimely death in 1887, before Mauriac's second
birthday, meant that, unless one believes strongly in inherited political
instincts, the subversive forces of that side of the family had little
chance to do him much damage. Politically, his was a world in which
he saw grown-ups vote very much as the curé would have them vote.
When their current monarchist favourite, the marquis de Lur-Saluces,
lost his seat to an upstart Republican lawyer, this débâcle was seen as
'la défaite de l'Église'.[13]

In many cases the preference for a monarchical instead of for a
republican regime was based on prejudice and family tradition. But
to thinking Catholics, the Republic's antagonism to their Church
made it necessary to discover a contrary ideology, a doctrine to make
their reaction intellectually respectable. They found it in the writings
of Charles Maurras and in the monarchist movement that sought to
realise his hope of the overthrow of the republican and democratic
edifice. Bordeaux was to become, between the two world wars, a
stronghold of the Action Française, to which even the Archbishop of
Bordeaux during that later period, Cardinal Andrieu, was to be
sympathetic.[14] Already, before the war, many young men of Mauriac's
social class sprang to the support of Maurras, among them Pierre
Mauriac, the eldest child of the family and later *doyen* of the notoriously Maurrassian Bordeaux Medical Faculty. There is no direct
evidence of what François Mauriac thought, as a youth, of the Action
Française. But in that the movement stood for a return to the old
values of order and discipline and for the pre-eminence of the family
group over the interests of the individual, it represented a type of
bourgeois orthodoxy which may well have not been to his liking.
The very popularity of the Action Française among young Catholics,
who saw it as a natural band-wagon on which to climb, may have
deterred an adolescent who was already very much his own man.
Evidence of the young Mauriac's independent temperament exists in

the form of an unpublished play called *Le Bon jeune homme, son maître et sa maîtresse*. This manuscript, which is to be found in the *Fonds Mauriac* of the Bibliothèque littéraire Jacques Doucet, seems to have been written when Mauriac was about seventeen: that is the age of the play's hero, with whom the author identifies himself very closely. The concerns it reveals are ethical rather than political: it satirises the over-valuation of sexual purity (startlingly so in view of Mauriac's later austerity), criticises the over-reaction to the alleged dangers of 'literature' and exposes the superficial religion of many so-called Catholics; but it contains one telling political point, a comment by the hero to his parish priest that the Church is more concerned to mobilise anti-Republican voters than to exterminate sin. This hardly makes of Mauriac, as yet, a political rebel, but it indicates a willingness to ask questions and look beyond the limited horizons of his family.

His literary mentor at this stage was a writer often associated with Maurras, sharing his patriotism and nationalist fervour though not his faith in a monarchical solution, but who had a passionate belief in individual values that evoked a ready response in Mauriac. This was Maurice Barrès, whose influence on him had so many ramifications, literary as well as political. A very selective approach is required, in this present study, to isolate this latter category, but the name of Barrès will recur so often in these pages than an outline of Mauriac's general reaction to him and to his work may be helpful. The first contact came with the discovery by Mauriac of a striking similarity of childhood experience between Barrès and himself. In the 'Oraison' at the end of Barrès' novel *Sous l'œil des barbares* he found an expression of unhappy memories of schooldays that reminded him very much of his own.[15] And in the reaction to the outside world and to other people of Philippe, hero of *Le Culte du moi*, he recognised the same wounded pride, the mingled feelings of strength and vulnerability, the determination to prove his worth as an individual, of which he himself was so conscious.[16] Barrès, he once wrote, was more than a mere literary master. He had prevented him from losing heart in a family milieu in which his individuality went unrecognised. He was the model on which Mauriac could base the opposition of his own self to the 'barbarians' around him.[17] The coincidence of this discovery of Barrès with his own adolescent rebelliousness gave Mauriac an attitude to life, or perhaps encouraged attitudes already burgeoning within him. His cherishment of the inner life was strengthened, his conviction of the primacy of personal values reinforced. In the short term he found in Barrès a spur to his own writing; stylistic similarities between his early writings and the works of Barrès have been observed by several critics.[18] But what did Mauriac think of Barrès the politician, one-time Boulangist deputy for Nancy, or of Barrès the nationalist myth-maker and political novelist?

An attempt to answer this question is bedevilled by the fact that Mauriac's most substantial account of his relationship with Barrès was published in 1945. Barrès' death twenty years earlier had ensured that, unlike many fellow nationalists, his reputation as a patriot had not been directly sullied by involvement with Vichy; in any event, had he lived until 1940 or beyond, his violent anti-Germanism would surely have made him a fierce opponent of Pétain's truce. Neverthe-less, in 1945, it was unfashionable, to say the least, to admit allegiance, past or present, to such a giant among nationalist ideologues, in whose support for the demagogic General Boulanger many saw as a pre-figurement of sympathy for modern Fascist dictatorship. Mauriac, at the time, was eager to ally himself with the forces of democracy and would scarcely wish, for all his admiration of Barrès, to remind his public of any role the latter may have played in his political for-mation. The Barrès he admired, he wrote, was the writer, the author of the *Culte du moi* trilogy, of *L'Ennemi des lois* and *Les Déracinés* and of the short fictional work *Un amateur d'âmes*. To almost all that Barrès wrote later, he paid respectful homage, in gratitude to what the man had given him; but these later works, he insisted, had not touched him. He observed with mere pity (*attendrissement*) Barrès' career as nationalist orator, struck by the irony of the man's transition from apologist of individualism to propagandist of collective values. 'Il s'offrait à la Cité en sacrifice', he wrote:

> L'homme libre consentait au sort d'Iphigénie. Son secret,
> il l'avait livré à quelques jeunes gens, dont j'étais le plus obscur,
> et maintenant il se battait au créneau, avec les barbares, contre
> d'autres barbares.[19]

Such an account is hardly satisfying. It plots the dividing line between admiration and mere respect for Barrès after the first volume of the *Énergie nationale* trilogy and before the more intensely political novels *L'Appel au soldat* and *Leurs figures*. As Mauriac must have realised, this distinction is a very dubious one. Barrès' devotion to a public cause was not so inconsistent with his view of individual liberty as Mauriac's rather facile jibe about Barrès' 'sacrifice' implies. The idea that the individual can only fulfil himself completely by identification with a collectivity based on race, place and time is as vital an element of *Un homme libre* and *Le Jardin de Bérénice* (which make up the *Culte du moi* trilogy with *Sous l'œil des barbares*) as it is of the later *Bastions de l'Est* or *La Colline inspirée*, while *Les Déracinés*, although political themes are less central in it than in the reconstructions of the Boulanger Affair and Panama Scandal in the two novels that follow it, cannot be fully grasped outside of its political context. So avid a reader of these early books as Mauriac could not be unaware of where their author stood politically. This does not necessarily mean that to admire them involved acceptance of his ideals; but Mauriac fails to prove rejection of Barrès' political views in his over-simple contrast between the early works and the later ones. The best evidence—indeed, the only evidence that exists—of Barrès' ideological influence on Mauriac is in the lecture on 'L'Idée de Patrie' in which, it was seen, Mauriac spoke of duty to the fatherland in unmistakably Barrèsian terms. He quite clearly shared Barrès' patriotism. That he did not yet, apparently, subscribe to his scornful view of parliamentarians and of the Third Republic's version of democracy may be due to another influence that ran concurrently (if conflictingly) with that of Barrès: namely, the influence of Marc Sangnier's Sillon. There will be much more to say about Barrès later, but in the meantime this other aspect of Mauriac's early experience demands attention. That he was a member of the Sillon is a matter of common knowledge, but the nature and duration of its impact upon him are such controversial issues, in the light of his later stress on the importance of this phase of his life, that a full study of his relationship with the Sillon is necessary at this point.

The Sillon was an interlude in a history of liberal Catholicism dating back to Lacordaire and Montalembert at the time of the July Monarchy and stretching forward to the formation of the Mouvement Républicain Populaire in the aftermath of the Second World War. It belonged to a tradition of reconciliation between Catholicism and the modern world that contrasted sharply with the intransigent outlook of the majority of Catholics at the turn of the century. 'La société moderne', writes René Rémond, 'inspire au catholique libéral sympathie, bienveillance, indulgence et volonté de compréhension; le catholicisme intransigeant ne se sent pour elle que défiance et suspicion.'[20] In the Sillon's case openness to modern society was manifested by the commitment to a reconciliation of democracy and Christianity and to the establishment of a new, practical interest in social problems on the part of Catholics. It campaigned for social reform and was especially active in the field of popular education. Workers were welcomed to its *cercles d'études*, sub-divisions of a dozen members, and were encouraged to participate fully in discussions rather than listen passively to their intellectual superiors as had been the case in earlier Catholic social movements like the paternalistic Œuvre des Cercles.[21] The Sillon had been founded in 1894 but increased rapidly in size and prestige from 1902 under Sangnier's leadership. By 1904 it had won the backing of Rome, which saw it as a key development in the possible success of the Ralliement. But just three years earlier Leo XIII's Encyclical *Graves de Communi* had hinted at misgivings towards Catholic action groups whose activities might be too overtly secular and political. It had rejected the term 'socialisme chrétien', accepted that of 'démocratie chrétienne' only in a specifically apolitical sense, and preferred to either of them 'action chrétienne populaire'.[22] These reservations limited in advance the Sillon's margins of action, and it soon ran into trouble. The Church hierarchy was worried by the absence of members of the clergy from the group's central committee, and these doubts increased from 1905 with Sangnier's declaration that the Sillon was essentially a lay organisation, free to act independently of the Church and free above all to campaign against Catholic electoral candidates if their politics were 'reactionary'. The growing political will of the Sillon, fired by Sangnier's own leftwards evolution, finally brought the papal censure of 1910. To this Sangnier yielded and, although he himself sought other platforms for the expression of his views, the Sillon was disbanded.

While it lasted, however, it drew enormous support from young Catholics, especially from the working classes which its educational schemes and agitation for reform were designed to help. But it sought intellectual recruits also, and that Mauriac was one of them was a fact that he never let the world forget. His motives in joining have never been objectively analysed. The general context in which to understand them is his interest in the Modernist crisis which was then current in the Catholic Church. This crisis centred on doctrinal issues, on new philosophies of immanence and inner revelation which opposed the official neo-Thomist thought of the period, and on the application to biblical exegesis of modern techniques of historical and textual research. The Sillon, in that it shared the desire to modernise Catholic attitudes, was a social equivalent of this current, a 'social modernism', to borrow the title of Mgr. Harscouet's hostile book on the subject.[23] Both forms of Modernism were to meet the same fate, for the 'errors' of doctrinal Modernism were condemned in the Encyclical *Pascendi* of 1907. Mauriac often expressed sympathy with some of the Modernist writers; their influence on his religious outlook and, more importantly, on his presentation of religious themes in his novels, has yet to be studied. It is conceivable that this sympathy—for Laberthonnière and Blondel, though not for Loisy[24]—and his interest in Foggazzaro's novel *Il Santo*, much read in Sillonist circles[25] and put on the Index in 1906, created in him a general willingness to listen to the views of Sangnier. His romantic attachment to the memory of Lacordaire and Montalembert, in whose relationship lies one of the sources of the many tender and idealised friendships which his novels portray, must also have contributed to a latent sympathy for liberal Catholicism. His sentimental admiration for the group of writers and reformers who met at La Chesnaie—Lamennais, Lacordaire, Montalembert and especially Maurice de Guérin—was such that he planned at one stage to write a history of their venture that might rival Sainte-Beuve's *Port-Royal*.[26] That he should associate in this way the men of La Chesnaie with the Jansenists of Port-Royal—the Catholic group which, above all others, possessed Mauriac's imagination—is a reminder also of his instinctive sympathy for minority organisations, especially persecuted ones, which must have lent further attraction, in his eyes, to the Sillon, fighting as it was against the tide of intransigence.

Emotional factors of this sort were undoubtedly uppermost in this aspect of Mauriac's early life. He stressed on numerous occasions the affective, rather than rational bases of his faith. The Sillon's relegation of theology to a secondary role, subservient to burning apostledom and the example of a pious life, was in keeping with this outlook. Equally appealing to the young Mauriac was the attitude of Sillonists to each other. 'Le Sillon est une amitié', Sangnier was fond of saying.[27] 'Tous les mouvements sociaux, politiques, religieux', Mauriac wrote later, clearly thinking of the Sillon, 'ont marqué notre époque dans la mesure où ils ont été des *amitiés*.'[28] In his case, his close personal friendship with the Sillonist André Lacaze was a determining factor in drawing him into the movement. Even more important must have been the influence of Mauriac's own brother Jean, who was studying at that time for the priesthood and who was as ardent a member of Sangnier's organisation as Pierre Mauriac, his and François' elder brother, was a supporter of Maurras and the Action Française. One of the paradoxes of Mauriac's autobiographical writings, explicable by his reticence to write directly about members of his own family, is

that, although so fond of dramatising the influences on his development, he makes no mention of this sharp contrast in his own home
between his Maurrassian and Sillonist brothers. He never refers, indeed, to Jean Mauriac's membership of the Sillon, the evidence of
which comes from the same important source of information as that
which reveals some of the details of François Mauriac's own Sillonist
experience.

Mauriac gave a partial account of his involvement with the Sillon
in a *bloc-note* of 1960,[29] but no actual written contribution to any
Sillonist publication came to light until my discovery of the three
pieces he wrote in 1905 for a paper called *La Revue fraternelle*.[30] These
were in fact his first published writings, and *La Revue fraternelle* was
the organ of the Bordeaux branch of the Sillon. Its first number relates
how that branch was established, initially in the rue du Commandant
Arnould and later, under the pressure of increasing numbers, in more
spacious premises at 4, rue de Lalande. There were at first some eighty
members, divided into eleven *cercles d'études*, and the group was supported by Cardinal Lécot, the predecessor as Archbishop of Bordeaux
of the Maurrassian Cardinal Andrieu. On one of his visits to Bordeaux,
Sangnier slept in the Mauriacs' grandfather's house in Langon. There
was, apparently, a certain clash of personality between the leader and
the younger Mauriac, a reminder of the latter's individual temperament
and possibly a portent of his eventual departure from the movement.[31]

The Sillon, opposed locally by the *Langon-Revue*, began to publish
its own monthly journal in Bordeaux, the first number appearing on
January 15th, 1905. The January and February issues contained the two
parts of a short story called 'Les Trois réponses', written by one J. M.
The February issue revealed the identity of this writer as Jean Mauriac
and described his speech at a recent meeting with the Sillon's Pau
branch. 'Les Trois réponses' is an interesting piece by virtue of the
image of the Bordeaux middle class which it presents. The hero reflects
on

> l'opposition malveillante des siens, leur crainte bourgeoise des
> idées avancées, la préoccupation mesquine d'un avenir à se faire,
> enfin tout ce christianisme de convention, odieuse caricature de
> celui que Jésus est venu nous enseigner et qui, sauvegardant les
> apparences, grâce à une pratique plus ou moins extérieure et
> pharisaïque, ne tend à l'amour idéal et au bonheur dans l'éternité
> que dans la mesure où cet amour ne compromet pas son bonheur
> dans le temps.

Had Jean Mauriac been projecting, by some gift of foresight, his more celebrated brother's portrayal of bourgeois Catholicism in his novels of the 1920s and 1930s, he could scarcely have been more accurate. The same scathing picture is painted by Jean Mauriac in the April issue, in an article called 'Esprit bourgeois et esprit de famille', which describes 'la complète indifférence de certains pour tout ce qui saurait troubler leur béate quiétude et leur sécurité matérielle'. On the question of the individual's relationship to the family, however, the same article expresses a clear belief that the family, in spite of its inhibiting conformity, is on the whole a beneficial influence, 'la seule force capable de lutter contre l'individualisme'.

The first five numbers of *La Revue fraternelle* contained no reference to Jean Mauriac's younger brother, but that of June 1905 included, together with a further article by Jean on 'Éducation démocratique', an account of a group pilgrimage to Lourdes, signed by *F. M.* That this was François Mauriac, a possibility already strongly suggested by the style of the writing, was confirmed by two later contributions, the short story 'La Tour d'ivoire', signed *François M*, which appeared in July, and the poem 'Intellectuels', bearing its author's full name on its publication in October. 'La Tour d'ivoire' is the most interesting of his three pieces for the paper. The protagonists, two schoolboys called Jean and Philippe, brought together 'par une égale horreur du foot-ball et par l'amour passionné des beaux vers', represent the first embodiment in Mauriac's work of idealised adolescent friendship. Philippe, a budding writer and determined individualist, expresses his ambitions in vintage Barrèsian terms (he even has the same Christian name as the narrator-hero of *Le Culte du moi*):

> Mon cher, je veux m'occuper de mon *moi*, le préciser chaque
> jour, l'enrichir en multipliant ses sensations et en fixant par
> l'analyse mes sentiments. Je veux développer ma personnalité, me
> distinguer de la foule inconsciente et barbare, et mon cœur sera
> un jardin clos que j'ouvrirai à une ou deux amitiés choisies.

Jean (Jean Mauriac?) argues that this is contrary to Christian charity, to which Philippe retorts that, since the world is irretrievably corrupt, communal effort is worthless. But a year later, when Philippe is disillusioned by his vain attempts to elevate his personality, Jean, now an ardent Sillonist, re-enters and gives meaning to his friend's life by introducing him to the movement. The narrative pattern of the story is thus identical to that part of Mauriac's first novel *L'Enfant chargé de chaînes* in which the hero Jean-Paul is persuaded to seek his salvation in the cause of Christian democracy. This common structure possibly owes its inspiration to the circumstances of Mauriac's own adhesion to the Sillon, but it should be pointed out that the introduction of an outsider by a member of the movement, a fairly obvious narrative device in any case, is a feature of other examples of Sillonist fiction such as Georges Hoog's novel *Rédemption* and the story 'Objections intérieures' which Louis Cazaubon contributed to the August 1905 number of *La Revue fraternelle*.

If the manner of the hero's joining the Sillon prefigures *L'Enfant chargé de chaînes*, so do his reactions to his experience as a member:

> Philippe se trouva troublé profondément, mais il songea qu'il ne pouvait approuver aujourd'hui ce dont il riait tout à l'heure. Une horreur le prit des grands mots qu'il croyait vides et de l'enthousiasme à froid. Il songea que sa foi agonisait dans son cœur. Et comme au fond il aimait sa tristesse et goûtait la volupté d'un facile mépris pour les hommes, il quitta Jean et orgueilleusement s'enfonça dans la nuit.

It is somewhat surprising to see such a challenging view of the Sillon finding expression in the group's own paper, but no doubt the implicit criticism of Philippe's attitude ('facile mépris', 'orgueilleusement') was enough to answer any misgivings on the part of the editorial committee.

The poem 'Intellectuels' was Mauriac's last contribution to *La Revue fraternelle*. Probably, the tensions between intellectual and worker which the poem reflects, as well as the disparaging opinion of Sillonist rhetoric expressed in 'La Tour d'ivoire', explain his lack of further participation. Once he had left Bordeaux for Paris, in 1906, he wrote nothing further for any of the Sillon's papers. Yet paradoxically there is evidence to show that, even after his arrival in Paris, he let himself be identified as a man sympathetic to Sangnier. He later described how he participated in the ideological battles that raged within the Réunion des Étudiants. Of his eventual election to the presidency of the Réunion he commented: 'C'était la victoire de la tendance sillonniste sur les tenants de l'Action Française.'[32] But there is some confusion in his account, for the date of the election, which he states as 1907, is revealed by an examination of the Réunion's paper *La Revue Montalembert* to have been November 24th, 1909. This is later than the date he gives elsewhere as that of his final departure from the Sillon, which took place, he says, in 1907.[33] But if the explanation he gives of his reasons for abandoning the Sillon is correct—it was due to the influence, he says, of his friend Jean Delouis, a disciple of the abbé Desgranges who led the Limoges branch of the Sillon out of Sangnier's organisation—this last date must also be wrong, as the schism described occurred in 1908. It would be pedantic to take Mauriac to task for errors in dates that have no great importance in any case. But these errors suggest that his own accounts of the period are unreliable, and warn against the over-estimation of his ideological commitment at that time. Possibly his initial dislike for the Action Française led him to support its Sillonist opponents in spite of his mixed experience in their Bordeaux circle. But whether his election as president of the Réunion can be accepted as a victory for the Sillon is very doubtful. Maurice Martin du Gard, a fellow resident, portrays it as a protest vote following Mauriac's expulsion from the residence as a result of over-zealous patronage of Latin Quarter bars.[34] This version is not without its ring of truth.

Whatever the precise chronology of events, the principal question remains. What was the nature of the Sillon's impact on Mauriac? Was it in any sense political? To answer this question, it is necessary to decide first of all in what sense if any the Sillon can be seen as a political movement. 'On n'a jamais su effectivement', writes one observer, 'et les Sillonnistes eux-mêmes ne l'ont peut-être jamais su, si le Sillon était un mouvement religieux à tendances sociales, ou politiques, ou un mouvement politique d'inspiration religieuse.'[35] The Sillon's commitment to establish Catholic involvement in a modern democratic society, its determination to prise apart concepts that had hitherto been seen as inseparable—Catholicism and Monarchism, Republicanism and anti-clericalism—were beyond doubt. But in view of Mauriac's constant stress on the crucial influence of Sangnier's goup on his development as a liberal, even 'left-wing' Catholic, other questions must be asked along with the previous one. In what precise way is the Sillon's defence of democracy to be understood? And how far, in its opposition to the Maurrassian Right, did it stand to the Left?

Jean de Fabrègues has shown that in its early period, up to the turn of the century, there was nothing that could be termed leftist about the Sillon. It believed firmly in the sanctity of private property and condemned socialist opponents of this tenet of bourgeois faith. In industrial affairs, it favoured corporatism and praised the integrity of the *patrons* whom it saw as having the natural leading role in a corporate system. It correspondingly denounced strike action and syndicalist agitation of any sort. Internationally, it was hostile to pacifists and enthusiastic about France's colonial expansion. And the Dreyfus Affair saw its already firm faith in the Army develop into a hatred of Zolaist intellectuals who dared to cast doubt on its leaders.[36] This scene had no doubt greatly changed, because of Sangnier, by the time Mauriac joined the movement. Yet there was still uncertainty about its political content, or whether it even had one at all. The editor of the first number of *La Revue fraternelle* stressed the democratic nature of the Sillon's programme, but care must be taken in interpreting this word. It could be, and was, used without any precise political meaning, as Paul Renaudin, Sangnier's predecessor as leader, had admitted. 'Si nous nous appelons démocrates,' he wrote, 'ce n'est pas parce que nous adoptons telle doctrine sociale (...) mais parce que ce mot nous paraît désigner l'état d'esprit de ceux qui aiment le peuple, qui ont compris sa misère et sa grandeur.'[37] This imprecise moralism was a feature of Sillonist democracy as late as 1905. 'La démocratie', wrote Fernand Germain in the February 1905 number of *La Revue fraternelle*, 'est le gouvernement qui exige le plus de vertus et qui réclame la force morale la plus puissante.' It was allied to a certain pragmatism, an acceptance of democracy as a *fait accompli*, not necessarily politically superior to any other system but simply here to stay, a historical reality. Catholics, unless they were to lose their stake in society, had to recognise this and prove their ability to work within the system. To the idealist Sangnier Catholic involvement was necessary to improve the quality of democracy: 'La démocratie ne suivra sa voie et n'accomplira sa mission', he wrote, 'que si elle est chrétienne et il faut dire plus: que si elle est catholique.'[38] But this general commitment fell short of political action. As a Bordeaux member wrote: 'Le Sillon ne se lance pas dans la politique: en cette matière, nous avons bien des conceptions précises, mais nous nous sommes toujours interdit la participation active aux luttes et aux débats électoraux.'[39] Sangnier himself told an audience of three thousand, during one of his trips to Bordeaux, that his personal support for syndicalism was conditional on its aloofness from the class struggle.[40]

Such was the Sillon that Mauriac joined: an apostolic movement devoted to popular eduction and apparently resolved to retain the innocence of which political embroilment might rob it. As such, it could and did attract men with no shadow of sympathy for left-wing ideas, men like Robert Vallery-Radot, intimate friend of Georges Bernanos and, like him, close to the Action Française. But the Sillon that Mauriac left was different. Sangnier's fast-growing political ambitions, his increasing part in electoral debates, had taken the movement with him on the road to papal censure. An important turning point was the discussion with the Action Française, which, at first surprisingly cordial, reached a point of overt and irrevocable hostility in 1906. Sangnier was henceforth to define his thought in opposition to that of Maurras, and this involved him in a clearer pro-Republican stance than before. In 1907 the launching of 'le plus grand Sillon', a wider movement which welcomed non-Catholics and even non-Christians, increased the rumblings of discontent among conservatives. Also, Sangnier's not very diplomatic gestures of tolerance towards Radical politicians who were remarkably short of that virtue in their dealings with Catholics—he even spoke from the same platform as Émile Combes on one occasion in 1908—caused his support from Catholics to weaken. There seems little doubt that to remain a member of the Sillon in the years between 1905 and 1910 meant lending support, however tacitly, to increasingly progressive political views. Mauriac's degree of willingness to do so is difficult to ascertain. It has been seen that his lecture on 'L'Idée de Patrie' expressed support for democracy and agreement, on the issue of patriotism, with Jaurès. But if his departure from the Sillon really was determined, as he said, by that of the abbé Desgranges, then it follows that he was obedient to the orthodox clerical view, anxious at the growing politicisation of the movement. The evidence, admittedly incomplete, is such as to suggest that he abandoned the Sillon because of its too overtly progressive trend.

So Mauriac's path and that of Sangnier diverged, not to cross again until both men were honoured guests at M.R.P. meetings in the 1940s. Sangnier's development after 1910 need not be traced here. However, his unhappy fate casts a piercing light across the world of Catholic politics and reveals the kind of obstacles that Mauriac himself would have to face in his own subsequent political evolution. Here was a man holding gradualist socialist views of the most moderate and humane nature, and yet who was prevented from expressing them from within an organisation that flew the banner of Catholicism; while at the same time a declared agnostic like Charles Maurras enjoyed support from many churchmen for his reactionary political creed. The contrasting situations of the two men illustrate the difficulty in practice of reconciling Catholicism with liberalism, and raise once again the question of the apparently natural affinities between Catholics and the political Right.

Meanwhile, as Sangnier was regrouping his cast on a secular stage, Mauriac was writing his first novel, *L'Enfant chargé de chaînes*, in which he drew on his Sillonist experience and presented in thinly disguised form his retrospective view of Sangnier's crusade. The account given above of his participation in the Sillon allows the novel to be seen in an even more directly autobiographical light than has been possible before. The inclination of the hero, Jean-Paul, towards Modernism, his regret at the Encyclical *Pascendi*, his refutation of neo-Thomism, his sense of the dangers of too close a relationship between Catholicism and power politics, embodied in the historical figure of Richelieu[41]— all of these traits, which exist in him before he joins the Christian democratic group Amour et Foi and which influence him to look favourably upon it in the first instance, he shares with his creator. Likewise, his introduction to the group by a close friend, the meetings in Bordeaux, the pilgimage to Lourdes, all are common to reality and fiction. Most intriguingly of all, the 'young man' who, after one of the group's meetings, accompanies the leader Jérôme Servet (an obvious caricature of Sangnier) to the house where a room has been prepared for him, 'dans cette petite ville dont Jérôme a oublié le nom'[42] (Langon?) may be a portrait in miniature of Mauriac himself, alongside the more obvious self-portrait that is Jean-Paul.

Other, more obvious borrowings from real life assured for the novel an immediate *succès de scandale*, especially the presentation of the Sangnier figure. The somewhat offensive physical protrait and the even more hurtful suggestion that Jérôme Servet had come virtually to replace Christ in the hearts and minds of his followers were eloquent testimonies to Mauriac's satirical talent. More seriously, he placed into the mouth of Servet's lieutenant, Vincent Hiéron, an expression of regret at the growing temporal ambitions of the Amour et Foi.[43]

It would be dangerous, however, to accept *L'Enfant chargé de chaînes* as a thoroughly reliable indication of Mauriac's opinion of the Sillon. It is not a document but a novel, and a relatively accomplished one at that, in which satire of the Amour et Foi is aesthetically and humorously balanced by censure of the man who rejects it. Like the story 'La Tour d'ivoire', the novel explores the hero's unsuitability for collectivist action. It stresses, as John Flower points out, 'his failure to mould his own nature to accept the movement's values'.[44] The chains that bind Jean-Paul are not of Servet's making. They are the restrictions of his own bourgeois refinement which leave him unable to bridge the gulf between himself and the working-class. Contact with workmen gives him the urge (shades of des Esseintes!) to 'se désencanailler' by garbing himself in exotically tinted pyjamas. Also, he has allowed literature to fence him in from the rest of life. His initially positive response to Servet is generated, characteristically, by literary associations (Servet's quoting from Pascal) and his attempted friendship with the workman Georges Élie disintegrates because the latter cannot discuss poetry with him. In the end, though, the influence of the Amour et Foi is a beneficial one, for it awakens in Jean-Paul an idealism that he hopes may be permanent even if social Catholicism is not the milieu in which it can flourish, and it reveals to him a sense of superiority which he realises he must combat. It is important to remember, when confronted with the disparaging references to 'les vieilles formules démocratiques' and 'les sauvages couplets de l'*Internationale*',[45] that these phrases reflect Jean-Paul's opinion. It is tempting, and possibly justified, to suspect that they reflect Mauriac's view also, but of that, on the evidence of the novel alone, one cannot be certain.

Indeed, although *L'Enfant chargé de chaînes* is certainly the best-known source of information on Mauriac's assessment of the Sillon, it is not the clearest or the most significant. More important is a little-known essay called 'L'Adolescence de Henri Lacordaire', published in 1920 in the volume *Petits essais de psychologie religieuse*. It describes Lacordaire's involvement with the Avenir group of liberal Catholics, led by Lamennais. This was the group that was widely recognised as a forerunner of Sangnier's movement. And while it is plain that Mauriac still felt great affection for Lacordaire the man and the priest, and was as touched as ever by his friendship with Montalembert, their support for liberal Catholicism is presented quite unequivocally, in this essay, as a youthful error on the part of the two men. Lacordaire is described as a naïve and impetuous youth, ruled less by reason than by the the passions of love and hate, an undiscriminating defender of liberties which he barely bothers to define.[46] But the real bite of the essay comes in the portrait of Lamennais. He is depicted as an embittered man, even unstable, capable of sudden joy and intense hatred, and his eventual banishment from the Church is seen not as noble martyrdom but as a self-inflicted exile into darkness. Mauriac's physical description of the man makes him appear sinister and repulsive, especially in contrast to the romantically portrayed younger members of his group, the 'marvellous' Maurice de Guérin, the pale Lacordaire wrestling with his destiny, Charles de Montalembert at the crossroads of his life. Lamennais, 'bilieux, violent et triste', dominates these young men, insists on their absolute loyalty to him as their leader. The values for which this unattractive and possessive man stands include the tolerance of new theological doctrines, an outlook which Mauriac himself had shared not many years earlier; and they include also those for which the Sillon had fought: the reconciliation of faith and modern thought, the separation of the Church from its traditional political alliances. But now these values are held suspect. In Lacordaire, salutary doubts are forming:

> Lacordaire déjà s'inquiète. Il craint d'enchaîner son coeur à ces idées, à cette philosophie qu'il accepte 'plus par lassitude que par conviction'. Seul, l'adolescent Montalembert, à l'âge où l'on aime admirer et s'humilier, lève un visage confiant vers son maître, ce rude homme qui, lui, ne met rien au-dessus de ses idées, pas même ses amis, pas même l'Église. Mais Henri Lacordaire, dans une lutte pathétique, arrachera son Charles à l'emprise de l'ange foudroyé.'[47]

To understand the significance of this passage and of the essay as a whole, one needs only to replace the names of Lamennais and the Avenir by those of Sangnier and the Sillon. The technique of destructive portraiture here is identical to that employed in *L'Enfant*. Lamennais, with his jealous dominance of his disciples as well as his unprepossessing personal appearance, is no less a deliberate caricature of Marc Sangnier than is Jérôme Servet. The image of Montalembert raising his head to gaze up in adulation at his master recalls the pose of the young admirer who walks home with Servet after an Amour et Foi meeting. And it is sufficient to make one further substitution of names —Mauriac for Lacordaire—to see that the essay embodies a curious allegory of Mauriac's experiences as a member of the Sillon. The Sillon is mentioned by name once in the essay, and is categorised along with the Avenir as one of 'les irréfléchies et généreuses croisades qui, à toute époque, ont ému la jeunesse croyante'.[48] Generous of heart but limited of mind—this is how Mauriac, in 1920, saw the Sillonists. His essay, more directly than his novel (because it is less of a fictional transposition), signals his severance from a movement to which he surely never expected to pay allegiance again. His frequent reiterations, many years later, of an unbroken line of fidelity to Christian democratic principles running from the Sillon to the M.R.P. must fail to convince in the light of such evidence. They imply a grossly exaggerated evaluation of the strength of his Sillonist commitment. At most, the Sillon may have introduced him to a range of political choices, an understanding of what the alternatives were for a young Catholic seeking a social and political stance. But he cannot realistically claim to have genuinely shared its outlook during or just after his association with the movement. Before the day dawned that would find him supporting the ideals of Christian democracy, Mauriac had a long and tortuous road to run, and at its end lay a new phase in his political life, not, as he wished to believe, simply a renewal of the old Sillonist one.

But what had happened to Mauriac between 1908 and 1920 that might explain his transition from a member of the Sillon, albeit a member of doubtful loyalty, to a critic of its supposedly unthinking outlook? The answer must be sought in his contact with other, opposing ideologies and personalities in the intervening period. For having found little to his taste in the ranks of the liberal Catholics, Mauriac, emerging from his rebellious adolescence, appears to have listened with some willingness to voices that emanated from more traditionalist areas of Catholic opinion.

(iii) *Mauriac and the Right, 1908–1920*

The picture thus far painted of the young Mauriac's somewhat superficial involvement in the social and political currents of his time is not meant as a criticism of any lack of consistency or stamina on his part. He had his intellectual wild oats to sow, and, especially after his arrival in Paris, he followed a deliberate policy of self-education by immersing himself in social environments of contrasting hues. He sought out Barrès and was introduced by him to the salon of Anna de Noailles, where the former Sillonist, fresh from his abortive attempt to cross social barriers in one direction, now did a complete about-turn. Among the personalities he met at the countess' gatherings were Proust, Valéry and Jules Lemaître, while his friendship with Lucien Daudet, brother of one of the Action Française's brightest talents, Léon, gave him access to the equally prestigious clan dominated by Mme Daudet, Alphonse's widow, where he made the acquaintance of Cocteau. Looking back on the apparent inconsistencies of his social activities during the years of early manhood, he marvelled at his ability to live on several planes at once, to adapt himself to whichever milieu he found himself in, without feeling the need to state a preference or make a choice. The inability or unwillingness to choose, which led him on the one hand to support Catholic literary groups like the Amitié de France while admiring the aggressively areligious literary opinions of the *Nouvelle Revue Française* on the other, he attributed to the influence of a new star on his horizon: André Gide.[49]

But Mauriac could and did take stands, as he showed in his relationship with the Amitié de France, a group to which he devoted his energies during the last two years before the war. The Amitié had been founded in 1906 by Georges Dumesnil, professor of philosophy at Grenoble. It published its own quarterly review and also, from January 1912, a sister review called *Les Cahiers de l'Amitié de France*. Mauriac contributed chiefly to the latter and soon became its general secretary. The spirit of the Amitié was closer to that of the mainstream of the Catholic literary revival than any group with which he had previously been associated. It was fired by a missionary zeal in the defence of traditionalism against new currents of thought, within and without the Church. Dumesnil summed up its aims as 'défendre, restituer et maintenir, autant qu'il sera en nous, la philosophie dont notre civilisation vit depuis deux mille ans'[50] and he saw, amongst the enemies of this ancient faith, not only the various non-Christian philosophies of the day but Modernist notions as well. He attacked the new theories in which, he said, 'Dieu subit l'exil, très souvent dans la forme habile de la relégation à l'intérieur'.[51] It says a great deal for Mauriac's adaptability that, despite his declared sympathy for the philosophers of Immanence, he could join forces with the holder of such a view. Perhaps, once again, he was swayed more by friendship—this time for Robert Vallery-Radot, who introduced him to the Amitié[52]—than by ideas.

As in the case of the Sillon, the attitudes of the Amitié de France towards doctrinal matters were also a guide to where its leaders stood politically. In Jean de Fabrègues' words, the group was 'fort certainement très orienté à droite'.[53] Vallery-Radot himself was soon to gravitate towards the Action Française, while another well-known name in the Amitié's ranks, the novelist Emile Baumann (yet another former Sillonist), was clearly a man of the Right. Indeed, simultaneously with his contributions to the Amitié, he was on the editorial board of the nationalist review *L'Indépendance*. As for the closest of all Mauriac's friends, inside or outside the Amitié, André Lafon, he was currently working on his novel *La Maison sur la rive*, which was to reveal an equally conservative social outlook. Whether Mauriac's attitude to the opinions of his fellow members went beyond mere tolerance, it is difficult to ascertain. His writings for the group's two papers were of a purely literary nature—poems and reviews—and reveal nothing of his political sentiments. But a reference in an article which he contributed to *La Revue hebdomadaire* in 1912 shows how far he had diverged from Sangnier's willingness to accept even the Combist laws: these 'persécutions jacobines', says Mauriac, had taught young Catholics the need to take up arms in the defence of their faith.[54] This view corresponds very closely to André Lafon's indignant reflections on secularisation in the novel already mentioned.[55]

In those years before the First World War, the acid test of how far a Catholic intellectual leaned to the Right lay in his attitude towards the Action Française, which enjoyed the support of a majority of conservatives. Here, in Mauriac's case, is an issue at least as controversial as his Sillonism. His denials of admiration for Maurras have been described. But Eugen Weber, in his history of the Action Française, portrays him as a man who 'had to battle constantly against a latent sympathy for the royalist movement'.[56] And Fabrègues, describing the tidal wave of Action Française support, says, 'A tout ce grand courant, même des hommes comme Mauriac d'un côté, Valéry de l'autre, ne restaient pas indifférents.'[57]

To determine any individual's degree of attraction to the ideas, aims and ethos of this most important of French nationalist movements is a complex matter. Like the Marxism which it abominated, like the ideas of Rousseau, Kant, Nietzsche and Freud which it identified as prime sources of moral erosion, the doctrines of the Action Française had so permeated the currents of thought of its time that men came to accept its ideas and share its aspirations without even reading a word of Maurras or of any of his disciples, or without even realising that the views they held were essentially Maurrassian. And the converse is also true: to establish that a man read *L'Action Française*, even on a regular daily basis, is to prove little of his political affiliations. Anyone interested in current affairs had to acquaint himself with the views of the paper, while the articles of Maurras, of Bainville, perhaps above all of Léon Daudet, put it into a class of its own as far as literary qualities were concerned, and drew readers from all parts of the political spectrum.

The catchment area of the Action Française's doctrine was also wide-ranging. A monarchist movement drawing massively on Catholic support, it nevertheless had the sympathy of many authoritarian Republicans and non-Catholics; Maurras himself made no secret of his agnosticism. Despite its denunciations of the Reformation and its fierce anti-semitism, its ranks included Protestants and Jews. Regardless of its supposed scorn for the professional and commercial middle classes as, historically, the originators of modern democracy, many people from these very milieux flocked to it. It was quite easy, therefore, for almost anyone of authoritarian temperament, with patriotic and traditionalist sentiments, suspicious of centralised bureaucracy, hostile to parliamentary 'talkers' who never got around to acting, or afraid of 'socialist' designs on his bank balance, to find some common ground with the Action Française. If that man were a Catholic, the enemies of Maurras and those of the Church could seem identical: they were the Republicans who had spent much of the two decades before the war persecuting the Church; and thus the Action Française came to dominate Catholic politics. Again, a morally conservative man, concerned about the declining values of contemporary society, could easily identify with Maurras' strictures on undisciplined individualism and on the falling prestige of the family as a bulwark of social order. Or a literary man, especially he who admired France's great classical tradition, might cling to the Action Française's literary doctrines as a last defence against romantic excesses. Men of one or all of these persuasions could be found within the movement, or else preferred to admire it from afar and be swayed by its advice at election time. Even when major differences of opinion on precise issues prevented close adhesion, the Action Française, in its general long-term aims and ideals, could appear as a pinnacle on the egalitarian plateau, a last hope of resurrection for a lamented epoch of hierarchical order.

What of Mauriac's attitude? Intellectually, this 'parti de l'intelligence', as it called itself, could not have failed to impress him more than the Sillon had done. Reading its paper, as he admits to doing, must have convinced this young man from a prejudice-ridden background, perhaps for the first time, that to be a reactionary was not necessarily proof of mental debility. And with whatever horror he witnessed, after 1940, the collaboration with the enemy of many actual or former Action Française sympathisers, he never doubted the sincerity of its patriotism in the years up to the end of the First World War.[58]

There were aspects of the movement's activity, however, that were bound to attract him less. It believed in Order, not necessarily in short-term orderliness; one can imagine what the somewhat sickly and disdainful aesthete, who had found the turbulence of the school playground distinctly repellent, thought of the Camelots du roi, the student pressure-group whose zeal in the service of the Action Française extended to physical intimidation of their opponents.[59] This bodily violence was paralleled, in the movement's paper, by a no less excessive verbal denigration of all enemies and by a dogmatic assertion of the truth of its own viewpoint. On the intellectual self-satisfaction of Maurras' band, its élitist superiority over less intelligent mortals, Mauriac left clear evidence of his opinion. He quoted in his diary, in the spring of 1914, a superbly ironic comment by Léon Bloy on the nineteenth-century apologist of Catholic order, Bonald, to the effect that the latter had apparently had no qualms at all about reproving three-quarters of the world's population (those alien to his concept of civilisation); applied to the Action Française, wrote Mauriac, this reflection 'annihilated' Maurras' movement.[60]

But it was in the totally different religious attitudes of Maurras and Mauriac that lay the widest gulf between them. Maurras was deeply suspicious of the anarchical and subversive elements that he saw in Christianity. As he reveals in his *Trois idées politiques*, he regarded intense religious belief as not only a rival to patriotic fervour but also a potential enemy of community values. To an individual opposed to the social hierarchy, opposed to the authority of family, race and fatherland, a personal God with whom to isolate himself could be a source of strength and thus endanger the cohesion of the group. 'Tel est le multiplicateur immense qu'ajoute l'idée de Dieu au caprice individuel', he says disparagingly.[62] He conceded that the Reformation had heralded a return to the spirit of primitive Christianity, but argued that this had been to the detriment of society. Protestantism incorporated the individualism that he so detested, while Catholicism had purified ancient Christianity of its oriental, barbaric and anti-social elements, establishing an intermediary structure between Man and God that channelled religious zeal in a direction propitious to social order. 'Le mérite et l'honneur du catholicisme', he insisted, 'furent d'*organiser* l'idée de Dieu et de lui ôter tout ce venin.'[62] So, like his ideological forebear Joseph de Maistre, Maurras ultimately saw the Roman Church as primarily an institution that encouraged order; and he went as far, in his avowed agnosticism, as seeing God as the finest creation of civilised Man. 'Il serait sans doute exagéré', comments Micheline Tison-Braun, 'de dire que Maurras voyait dans l'amour de Dieu un obstacle à l'accomplissement de la fonction sociale de l'Église, mais il n'en faisait certes pas la condition nécessaire.'[63]

To Mauriac, with his profound faith, these ideas were repulsive.

'Quand Charles Maurras prétendait trouver dans l'Église romaine la meilleure défense contre le venin du *Magnificat*,' he once wrote, 'cela nous paraissait horrible, à nous qui croyions que l'Église catholique est ce grand arbre né du grain de sénevé que le Seigneur est venu jeter dans le monde.'[64] Social order was nothing compared to the inherent truth of the Christian message. If Mauriac had been presented with proof that Jesus was not the Son of God and that there was nothing divine in the Church of Rome, he would have renounced his faith in disgust, he said, 'dût la société s'écrouler sur mes épaules'.[65] In this diametrical difference between Mauriac's faith and the insistence of Maurras on the primarily social role of the Church (which Barrès, too, very largely, shared), lay the greatest obstacle of all to Mauriac's adhesion to the Action Française. It might be argued that his many references to the Maurrassian 'positivists',[66] to 'les sectateurs d'un Dieu sans mystique',[67] all date from the post-Vichy period and were made with an eye to political convenience. But as early as 1916, in his war-time diary, Mauriac was declaring his opposition on this crucial point, and expressing a preference, as far as religion was concerned, for the defeated Sillonists, rather than for the atheist who had benefited, in terms of Catholic support, from the condemnation of Sangnier's movement.[68]

It says a great deal for Mauriac's fairness and for his willingness to distinguish between different planes of argument that this vital, ineradicable difference did not lead him to reject *en bloc* all that Maurras stood for. The diary which he kept throughout the war contains so many references to Maurras that the interest the latter held for him is clear. From around 1916 the entries in the diary are notable for a new seriousness of political comment. It seems likely that it was the experience of war itself that led Mauriac to consider political and social problems with a new urgency, and in so far as his ideas began to form, now in opposition to Maurras, now in agreement with him, the latter was an educating force in Mauriac's life at this time. In his old idol Barrès he now expressed disappointment. Barrès, who had been provoking anti-German feeling for years in the hope of a holy war that would result in the retrieval of the sacred Eastern provinces from the enemy, ought to have been in his element as a persuasive wartime orator; but, wrote Mauriac, '(il) rate sa note à chaque instant'.[69] He was altogether too subtle and allusive to make much impact on the masses to whom he addressed himself.[70] They, like Mauriac, needed a new master. Did Mauriac see him, in potential, in the figure of Charles Maurras? 'C'est l'individualiste en moi qui est attiré par Maurras', he confided to his diary;

> (. . .) s'il l'emportait, l'individu serait sauvé du nivellement, l'intelligence de l'uniforme rudiment des Universités, la France de l'uniforme laideur administrative.[71]

He was certainly guilty here of misinterpreting Maurras' thought. Maurras was no friend of *individualists*, who were always likely to revolt against a hierarchy led by certain *individuals*, rightly privileged by birth. But he was closer to the mark in his identification of Maurras as an anti-egalitarian, and his expression of support for this outlook is unequivocal. It was followed by a diagnosis of France's fading military fortunes which, in its condemnation of parliamentarians who were mismanaging the conduct of the war, its regret at the absence of a dynamic leader, even its scorn for Maurras' *bête noire* Aristide Briand, could almost have been copied from an *Action Française* editorial of the period. The lesson Mauriac drew, as he looked ahead to an eventual post-war generation, was a reactionary and élitist one: 'Après la guerre, chacun sur son plan, travailler au groupement des meilleurs.'[72] France, he hoped, would emerge in peace-time as 'la grande force conservatrice et réactionnaire du monde'.[73]

Why should Mauriac, former Sillonist and one-time defender, as in his lecture 'L'Idée de Patrie', of democracy, now give such firm support to what was in essence a Maurrassian concept of France's future? The answer can only lie in the emotional stress of war, in the horror of 'l'oppressante, l'écrasante armée de nos quinze cent mille morts',[74] the loss of whom he was always to blame for France's inter-war weakness. The decimation of the 18th Corps from Bordeaux, which included old school-friends,[75] the death of close friends like Jean de la Ville de Mirmont and (though through illness) of Charles-Francis Caillard and of his beloved André Lafon were more personal shocks, aggravated by his own guilty feelings at being forced, by delicate health, to serve in an ambulance unit rather than in the front line with his comrades.[76] His reaction was to ask where the blame lay for the military weakness and strategic blunders that had allowed the war to last so long, and Maurras provided an answer that, to a man willing to be convinced, may have seemed plausible: in ineffectual democratic government, in a parliamentary system which perpetuated national divisions rather than uniting the nation in its common struggle. Certainly, Maurras' indictment of politicians for their inability to stop the mass slaughter was more in keeping with Mauriac's mood than the aggrandisement, by Barrès, of this war of revenge for 1870; and it helped to lead Mauriac to follow a growing trend among Catholics at that time and turn away from his old favourite towards the propagandist of integral nationalism.

There remained, as there would always remain, a stumbling-block: the exploitation of Catholic support by an agnostic in the interests of a purely temporal cause. The importance of this obstacle, which prevented a total and open expression of sympathy for Maurras, is revealed in Mauriac's *Petits essais*, written during and just after the war. They include the study of Lacordaire which embodies, as has been described, a rejection of liberal Catholicism. They contain also, in the essay on the Protestant writer Henri-Frédéric Amiel, criticisms of 'German' philosophers and of the reformed religion that Maurras would not have disdained. But in spite of this, they also present, in the final essay in the volume, a clear statement of divergence from Maurrassian doctrine. The essay in question, 'Henri Beyle et les revenants', begins with an expression of cultural chauvinism and of opposition to the 'American way of life' that to many conservative moralists threatened to submerge European traditions. Again, Maurras would not have demurred. But he would certainly have disagreed with the rest of the essay. Stendhal, whom Mauriac attacks, was greatly admired in Action Française circles for his cool brand of *Realpolitik*. But to Mauriac, pragmatism was the last lesson needed by a young man back from the war; though he need not reject the goal of the Stendhalian *chasse au bonheur*, he must seek to achieve that happiness within a spiritual dimension. Stendhal's indifference to religion was his greatest error, he went on, and this was true of his political as well as of his philosophical outlook, in his view of the Church as no more than the vehicle of temporal power. The application of this statement to the Action Française needs no underlining.

The essay encroaches on even holier Maurrassian ground than this. It was written, at least in part, during Mauriac's war service in Salonika, and his presence in Greece led him to meditate on the ideal of a pagan but structured and stable society, an ideal that had its roots there and to which so many modern thinkers subscribed. Nietzsche, Renan and others, he wrote, had their vision of a bright Athenian past, an age as yet undarkened by the shadow of the gibbet on which Christ was to die. Thucydides and Aristotle encouraged the concept of a harmonious hierarchy, an equilibrium dependent purely on social order. In this ideal many saw the prefiguration of the Church of

Rome, viewed not as a fountain of divine truth but merely as an institution. But was Athena's smiling face not merely a mask, behind which lay the anguish of an unredeemed world? Greek literature, argues Mauriac, betrays the anguish of Man devoid of God's love, and points to a gulf between Antiquity and Christendom that apologists of the Grecian ideal overlook. In seeing Roman Catholicism as simply the inheritor of a tradition of order, they neglect, as Stendhal neglected it, the spiritual plane. Catholicism had retained what was best in Greece but had rebuilt it on a bedrock of faith. And nowhere do the two traditions blend more perfectly than in France. The finest embodiment of their convergence is the humanist and Catholic Frenchman— Catholic in a spiritual as well as institutional way.

So far, in this impassioned analysis, Mauriac had not mentioned Maurras by name. He did not have to. It was well known that Maurras had brought back the bases of his social theory with him from a journey to Athens on the occasion of the first modern Olympic Games in 1896. Mauriac's readers would not fail to realise that the leader of the integral nationalists ranked prominently among the 'bien d'autres' whom he described as sharing Nietzsche's and Renan's adulation of Greece. And what Mauriac was saying was that Maurras, and all others who did not recognise that the spirit of Christianity, as well as the institution, was inseparable from French tradition did not understand the very race that they sought to elevate. French-ness included faith as well as the reason which Maurras admired in Greece. Maurras, says Mauriac, at last referring to him overtly, praised the victory, in Stendhal, of reason over passion; but Mauriac himself, as a Christian, would reformulate the stuggle—not just Stendhal's, but that of all men—as one of conscience against instinct. Here lay the vital difference, in spite of all the attraction of nationalist social and political ideas for Mauriac, between him and the philosopher of the Action Française.

By 1920, therefore, Mauriac had arrived at a maturely considered intellectual position. He stood unequivocally to the right of centre on the political scale, believing in an élitist society and in the need for France, in a world that now had the example of Leninist Russia before it, to emerge as a great conservative power, in the vanguard of anti-Bolshevik reaction. But for religious reasons he retained his independence, stood aloof from the movement whose members were the most vocal supporters of these same social and political views. It would be misleading, however, to present him, at this still relatively early stage in his life, as a man deeply involved in public affairs. Politics was not yet of central importance in his life. Over fifteen years had still to elapse before his emergence as a political commentator. In the meanwhile Mauriac had his first career ahead of him, the writing of the major novels which first established his importance in French literary life.

Chapter Two

MAURIAC AND THE DOCTRINES OF ORDER

(i) *Family, Nation and Place*

The 1920s and early 1930s were for Mauriac the greatest years in his life as an imaginative writer. This was also a time of personal anguish as he struggled to find a happier relationship between his Christian faith and his fear both of moral shortcomings and of exerting a morally harmful influence through his work. His writings—not only the novels, but also the essays and articles on religious and literary issues—were dominated by these problems, and direct references to social and political matters became very infrequent. This period appears, at first glance, to be a hiatus in the story of his political development. Jean de Fabrègues treats it as such, advancing rapidly from the end of one war to the eve of the next.[1] Nobody doubts that Mauriac held political opinions, but the lack of published evidence of what those opinions were has led biographers to dismiss the years of the major novels as not very fruitful ones from this point of view. Fiction and politics seem two separate areas in Mauriac's world, a notion which he himself encouraged by remarks like the one made by him to Madeleine Chapsal, on his involvement in the disputes over Spain: 'L'horreur du monde réel m'a chassé de la fiction.'[2] And even after his emergence as a political observer, he never became a political novelist in any obvious sense of the term. The inclusion among the secondary characters of his late novel *Le Sagouin* of a socialist schoolteacher and an Action Française journalist is no more significant than the marginal references, in *Thérèse Desqueyroux*, to the Republican sympathies of the heroine's father. Does it not follow, therefore, that Mauriac's novels, as well as his literary essays, are simply irrelevant to this present study?

33

They provide no information, it is true, on his detailed reactions to the events of the inter-war years. But, as this chapter sets out to show, they help in a very important way to throw light on his general social outlook. The essays, which plot the course of his moral uncertainty during these years, show him seeking support, almost instinctively, in orthodox moral attitudes which involve, by extension, conservative social beliefs. The novels, often in intellectual and emotional conflict with the essays, reveal the same tensions, but more ambivalently. The novel, as a genre, can be a fascinating guide to a writer's social standpoint regardless of its degree of precise political comment. For, speaking very broadly, political debate since the Revolution and the novel in France over the same period share a great common theme: the relation of the individual to the group and to the wider social collectivity. In modern pluralist societies, a stable balance between the liberty of the individual and the authority of the group has proved difficult to find, and the resultant tensions are the concern of many novelists, even when they approach the issue from a psychological or moral, rather than social or political angle. One can express this view in the Marxist terminology of a Goldmann:

> Le roman (est) un genre épique caractérisé (. . .) par la rupture insurmontable entre le héros et le monde.

> Il existe une homologie rigoureuse entre la forme littéraire du roman (. . .) et la relation quotidienne (. . .) des hommes avec les autres hommes, dans une société productrice pour le marché.[3]

Or else one can regard it as self-evident that the relation of the individual's values to those of his milieu is as typical a concern of the modern novelist as it is a central issue in the work of certain French social theorists. One of the main themes of Mauriac's novels—the situation of the individual within an unsympathetic family—involves an interrogation of the authority of the family as a group; this authority, in the writings of Maurras, is sacrosanct, the very basis of social stability. Here is an issue, therefore, which lends itself to a direct comparison of attitudes between Mauriac and the theorist with whom his intellectual relationship is so controversial. The gap between the two men's respective positions, up to 1920, a gap created by their religious differences, has been described. Whether it widened or narrowed in the inter-war years is a question which Mauriac's essays and novels help to clarify in quite unexpected ways.

To understand Maurras' veneration for the family, it is necessary to refer to the theory of the origins of society which can be extrapolated from his major writings. At the basis of that theory, in turn, lies an assessment of human nature which Maurras would have termed empirical but which was, in reality, fundamentally emotive. In his essay 'L'Homme', he rejects Aristotle's optimistic view of Man as a naturally altruistic creature and prefers that of Hobbes, which he sums up in the formula: 'L'homme est pour l'homme un loup.' Man's nature as hostile predator means that human relationships are built on natural enmity and on the dominance of the strongest. While men may forge friendly links, characterised by agreement or affection, such associations can never exist between individuals of equal strength. Like Crusoe when he first encounters Friday, Man's first instinctive reaction in the presence of a fellow man is fear and mistrust; his second, when he learns like Crusoe that his is the superior force, is to calculate how best to exploit this superiority and dominate the other. And reflection tells him that this dominance, this assumption by one man of leadership and by the other of subservience, will be in the interest of both parties. The most perfect illustration of mutually beneficial relationship between unequal collaborators, Maurras goes on, is the family, the natural social group on which all societies are founded. Man civilised himself, left the state of nature, controlled his environment because the members of his own family multiplied the strength of his arm. They did so out of respect and fear for their natural leader, the father. What Maurras proposes here is a paradigm of the feudal and paternalist systems, in which the energies of individuals are harnessed to the common good of themselves and the group. The basic inequality between father and son—power in the hands of the former, a blend of duty and self-interest in the minds of the latter—is to him the cement of society. Equality breeds decomposition.[4]

The family, acting as one man because one mind directs it, reverts to the instinctively hostile attitude of Man towards outsiders. Other groups spell danger and are to be kept at a distance. But the group may grow organically with the arrival of more offspring and the intake of fugitives, servants and prisoners of war, until a larger group forms, still held together by reciprocity of service. The more extensive the group and the more resistant to forces within and without that might upset its unity, the greater will be the security it offers to its members. Such groups can be of enormous size, Maurras allows; and in his book *L'Ordre et le désordre* he sees medieval Christendom as one such large family, now tragically dispersed. But the next best alternative to Christendom is the Nation, and that is why, in modern circumstances, unconditional patriotism is the duty of all right-minded men. 'La Patrie d'abord,' he insists. 'La France, sans *mais*, sans *si*, sans condition.'[5] So, to Maurras, opposition to the family and rejection of patriotic duty resolved themselves into one common attitude of mind. They were symptoms of the same rebellious spirit. He was scandalised that intelligent beings could oppose these honoured concepts, and he could scarcely believe in the integrity of those who did. 'Qu'il se trouve des idiots pour dire après cela: "Familles, je vous hais!"' he writes in his *Politique naturelle et politique sacrée.*[6] 'Ils ont eu rarement le front d'appliquer ce principe. Gide, qui le posait, l'a contredit à tous les instants de sa vie.' True social life, he argues in the same book, is built on the foundation-stone of the family. To weaken the family and society in the alleged interests of individual liberty is ultimately to the good of nobody.

So anti-individualism is a constant in Maurras' thought, alongside anti-egalitarianism. The doctrines of liberty and equality, enshrined in the revolutionary tradition, were to him incompatible with the third principle adorning the Republican banner: fraternity, the only one of the three to which he paid homage. But even fraternity he saw as attainable only within the harmonious framework of the organic nation state. 'Une patrie', he declares in *Mes Idées politiques*,

> est un syndicat de familles composé par l'histoire et la géographie; son principe exclut le principe de la liberté des individus, de leur égalité, mais elle implique, en revanche, une fraternité réelle, profonde, organique, reconnue par les lois, vérifiée par les mœurs, et dont le pourtour des frontières fait le signe matériel.[7]

Without self-discipline on the part of individuals, fraternity is impossible and so is national harmony. Nations are torn apart when diverse factional interests come into conflict, and that is why democracy, which not only tolerates but encourages dissident voices, is productive of disharmony. Democratically elected leaders, spokesmen by definition of the biggest faction at any given time, can never exert the appeal to the entire nation that had been the attraction and strength of hereditary monarchy. So in Maurras' system a thread of single-minded logic runs from respect for the family to belief in the virtues of monarchy. The child allowed to rebel against the will of his parents was likely to grow up into the 'democrat'—a term which to Maurras meant simply the holder of a partial viewpoint—whose disputes with other 'democrats' produced nothing but national instability.

A reader of Mauriac's novels would probably find them very remote, in their characteristic presentation of the family, from such views. Mauriac would seem to champion the individual in the struggle to free himself from family conformity. His role in the vanguard of the twentieth century's challenge to family values appears all the more assured in that, as a Catholic writer, he can be seen to carry the banner of individualism right into the stronghold of the enemy. Catholic novelists before him—Bourget, Bazin, Bordeaux, Jammes, as well as minor figures like Retté and Lafon—had all stoutly defended the family as a bastion of stability in a crumbling moral order, and in the novels of Bernanos also, the dissolution of family ties through lack of sacred charity is both cause and effect of a decaying civilisation. Mauriac has been heralded as the exception among Catholics. 'Il se crée,' says Micheline Tison-Braun, describing the development of the novel between the wars, 'un véritable roman noir de la famille, auquel Mauriac a donné son titre symbolique: Le Nœud de vipères.'[8]

The blows that Mauriac's novels deal in this combat are of varying weight, and their point of impact is not always the same. In the very early novels, the values of the family, associated with the life-styles of older people, like Jacques' grandmother in La Robe prétexte, are presented not as wrong but simply as unexciting to an adolescent with a thirst for the absolute. In Préséances, the satire on the family as an institution is blunted by the as yet immature author's uncertainty of tone, his disconcerting switches from the gross caricature of the 'Fils des Grandes Maisons' to the melodrama of the heroine's crisis of mysticism. A deeper note is struck in the final pages of Le Baiser au lépreux, where Mauriac portrays a young widow doomed to loneliness, partly because of the family's strictures on re-marriage. Its sequel Genitrix depicts a grotesque mother-son relationship, but the canvas, limited mainly to two individuals, includes no censure of the family group as such. Next comes Le Désert de l'amour, with its more ambitious portraits of a misunderstood son and a middle-aged father trapped in a loveless marriage.

None of these novels is as central to the subject of this part of the present study as Thérèse Desqueyroux. From the opening sequence of the novel, as Thérèse leaves the magistrates' court where the case against her (the alleged attempted murder of her husband) has been found non-proven, Mauriac almost provocatively engages his reader's sympathy for this victim of the family. In their eyes, she is no more than the bearer of the next generation of the Desqueyroux, denied any individuality of thought or action, and finally cast out like another social rebel before her, her grandmother, Julie Bellade. Thérèse, 'image brouillée de mes propres complications', says Mauriac,[9] was the vehicle of his outburst of resentment, in 1927, as he remembered the reduction of his individuality under the repressive influences of his family circle. 'Au collège, dans la famille,' he writes in *Bordeaux*, 'je faisais partie d'un tout, je n'existais qu'en fonction d'un groupe.' He was told: 'Le règlement est fait pour tous (. . .) Tu n'es jamais comme les autres (. . .) Tu n'es pourtant pas différent des autres (. . .) tu es fabriqué de la même pâte.'[10] His resentment, it is true, was of no precise social or political significance, but its expression in this novel suggests that temperamentally and by the nature of his experience Mauriac was not a man to listen to Maurras' passionate elevation of the family over the individual. Here, it would seem, is another obstacle between them.

There is a further area of Mauriac's work in which one can develop the notion of a temperamental gulf between him and not only Maurras but nationalist and conservative opinion generally: namely, in the concept of place. In the works of the Catholic authors mentioned above, attachment to family, nation and religion is often accompanied by attachment to a particular locality, usually the native region of the author. The novels of René Bazin and Henry Bordeaux illustrate this association, but it comes to its fullest fruition in the writings of the man who had introduced Mauriac, on the intellectual level, to the patriotic ideal: Maurice Barrès. The cultivator of 'le moi' had evolved in a manner that caused some early enthusiasts to cry 'Betrayal!' and other initial doubters to welcome him to the authoritarian fold. In truth Barrès did not so much reverse his position as develop it. *Enfant terrible* of nationalism, his view of the individual was more nuanced than that of Maurras, and his defence of community values was designed to produce, not an ideology to oppose individualism, but a guiding framework in which the individual, conscious of the gifts of race and place, could grow spiritually and culturally beyond his own limits, to the advantage of himself and the group. His *anti-déracinement* thesis, which urges men to spring from their natural roots, has none of the austerity or oppressiveness of the strictures on social mobility expressed in Bourget's *L'Étape*. It aims at providing a basis for individual fulfilment, an inner life in keeping with the rhythms and traditions of the native land. Such correspondences between inner and outer landscapes are already traced in *Le Culte du moi*, in the images of Lorraine and Venice and in the Aigues-Mortes which encapsulates the true nature of Bérénice. Further, more fully developed examples appear in the second trilogy of novels, especially in the presentation of Lorraine as the mirror of the soul of his seven *déracinés*. This sacred landscape has a civilising force, teaching the individual to love those qualities within himself that he shares with the race, and to beware of those which have a mere personal relevance, without the weight of tradition. And that this civilising force ultimately tends to the creation of the same paternal order dreamed of by Maurras and to the same respect for the family, is seen in St.-Phlin's decision, after his bicycle tour with Sturel of the beloved Eastern provinces, to settle in Lorraine, be 'un chaînon de la série lorraine', raise children '(qui) auraient des cerveaux selon leurs aïeux et leur terre'.[11]

Of the same St.-Phlin, Barrès writes in *Les Déracinés*, 'Décrire sa vie, toute intérieure, c'est décrire son pays qui seul l'anime.'[12] This identification of man with place has its equivalent in Mauriac's autobiographical writings too. 'L'histoire de Bordeaux', he writes, 'c'est l'histoire de mon corps et mon âme (. . .) Les maisons, les rues de Bordeaux, ce sont les événements de ma vie (. . .) Je l'aime, c'est-à-dire, je m'aime.'[13] Yet Mauriac's concept of geographical locality differs from that of Barrès and other traditionalist thinkers in a fundamental way. The key-note of Barrès' Lorraine is its harmony. It is before the moving spectacle of 'les harmonies de cette prairie'[14] that Sturel and St.-Phlin realise their spatial and temporal relationship to the province and its people, past and present. Harmonious landscape calls out to them to respect the old ways, those of the men who have lived on this soil. It projects an image of values greater than the self, putting into perspective the petty divisions of the moment and submerging the anarchic tendencies of men. But Mauriac's Guyenne, Mauriac's Bordeaux, are symbols not of harmony but of conflict. They are images of duality, not of unity. Memories of the lost paradise of childhood in Bordeaux ('le lieu où je fus pur'[15]) mingle with those of adolescent temptation, of the first terrifying encounter with sin: the red-light area of the Place Mériadeck, the Ash Wednesday carnivals in which 'chaque masque était à mes yeux un homme dans un état de péché'[16]; while the call of departure from the sirens of the boats anchored in the Garonne evoked dreams of discovery of the world and of the self that were simultaneously exalting and alarming.[17] Outside Bordeaux, too, in the countryside of the Landes, rival voices were heard beckoning to him: that of Christ and that of the pagan earth-goddess Cybele, that recurring symbol, in Mauriac's writings, of attachment to nature, obstacle to grace. 'Le Christ enseigne à nos âmes,' he writes,

> qu'il est la vigne et que nous sommes les sarments; mais Cybèle donne une même leçon à nos corps. C'est ainsi que (. . .) commençait un singulier combat qui ne devait finir qu'après bien des années. Est-il jamais fini?'[18]

Geographical oppositions furnish many writers with symbols of conflict which express the dialectical tensions within them. For Balzac as well as for Barrès the contrast of Paris with the provinces was a fruitful one. One of the reasons why the world of Mauriac's novels is so spatially limited is that Bordeaux and the Landes already provided him with an adequate image of dilemma; as an artist he needed nothing more. The duality of his imaginary Bordeaux points also to his profound Christian sense of a fallen world. His concept of landscape is a theological, almost manichean one, a reminder that his religion shaped his way of seeing the world more totally than the institutional Catholicism of a Barrès or a Maurras could shape theirs. As a polemicist, Barrès could point to a perfect Lorraine and contrast it with a diluted and cosmopolitan Paris. As a Christian moralist, Mauriac saw everywhere the mark of Man's dual nature. The struggle for moral order was an inner one, and no comfort could be found in the tainted mirror of external nature.

As for the second element in the Barrèsian cult of the earth and the dead—a willing inheritance of tradition based on respect for our ancestors—this, equally, was hardly likely to find an echo in Mauriac's Jansenist imagination. Inheritance, for Mauriac, meant inherited sin. Heredity is associated in his novels, symbolically, with weakness and decay. The old *génitrix* is no sooner dead than her gruesome traits reincarnate themselves in her pitiful son. All of this is far from the pride in family that characterises the outlook of Barrès and that of Maurras, too, who accepted gladly the family, milieu and traditions into which he was born. Mauriac, in contrast, would have approved of the definition of the family given by a younger, less community-conscious Barrès: 'ces relations que je ne me suis pas faites moi-même'.[19] He even expressed irritation at having been born into a Catholic family[20] and thus robbed of the chance to embrace the faith at a later age and by his own volition. He would have agreed with Louis, the hero of *Le Nœud de vipères*, that Christianity is worthless if it is a mere family heirloom. Inheritance is not enough.

All of this does not infer that Mauriac rejected Maurras, Barrès or any other traditionalist writer on the overtly political plane. He shared their patriotism, that much is certain. But it does mean that at a deep, imaginative and spiritual level there were elements within Mauriac's personality which might prevent him from being won over by a social outlook that laid so much stress on family and place. On the other hand, however, there were also deep fears in Mauriac which acted in the opposite direction and brought him nearer than has hitherto been imagined to these defenders of a traditional order. The context in which to explore these factors is Mauriac's, and Maurras', view of literature and its relation to society.

(ii) *Literary and moral order*

In Maurras' closely integrated (some would simply say narrow) system of thought, literature and politics overlap. The artistic products of an age being inseparable from the prevailing social and political conditions, most literature since the hated Revolution bore the mark of the beast. In his *Révolution et romantisme* of 1922, he argues that the two phenomena so confidently bracketed together in the title are the twin heads of the same monster. Sweeping aside the objections of all those writers (one of them was Balzac[21]) who protest that a division between revolutionary and counter-revolutionary cannot always be forced into easy coincidence with that between romantic and anti-romantic, Maurras insisted that his simple but lucid view was the correct one. He saw the Revolution and the Romantic movement as the indissolubly linked long-term results of the Reformation, which he described, borrowing Auguste Comte's formula, as 'une sédition systématique contre l'espèce'.[22] The sources of the Revolution that had destroyed what was best in French tradition were foreign ones, stemming from Swiss, German and, most sinister of all, Jewish culture. The annihilation of monarchical order and civilising classicism had come about through no less than an insidious invasion from the East. The true ancestor of the Revolution was Luther and the mentality of Germans in general—'l'empire de leur sensibilité imagée sur la raison indégrossie, la préséance du particulier sur le général, du privé sur le social'[23]—had contaminated French literature via Romanticism. France, in the seventeenth century, had had the good taste to shake off the barbaric influences of the Reformation that had corrupted Northern Europe; this was, indeed, the historical reason for the fine flowering of French classical culture, with its roots in Graeco-Roman antiquity. Resisting anarchy, France had founded the glories of her greatest century on royal absolutism, Catholic religion and on an art which reflected the stability of both. The contagion was renewed following the visits to Protestant England of Montesquieu and Voltaire: although they themselves did not catch the disease, they were the carriers of deadly germs which led to the epidemic of the so-called Enlightenment. This latter phenomenon and the ensuing Declaration of the Rights of Man were, Maurras argues in *L'Ordre et le désordre*, a complete deviation from the traditions of the Latin race.[24] Hard on their heels had come Revolution and Romanticism, in that order. The first Revolution had spawned the Romantic movement, said Maurras, and the latter had inspired in turn the later revolutions.[25] The literary weaknesses of Romanticism are the surest proof of the political error of the Revolution. The decadence of post-revolutionary times is enshrined in Romantic art. Indiscipline, misguided trust in individual judgment, rejection of the lessons of the past: these elements reign in both spheres.

Such was the onslaught on individualism, in literature and in society, made by Maurras and certain of his disciples, notably Pierre Lasserre, the author of *Le Romantisme français*.[26] The venom of these writers towards a movement which had declined by the second half of the nineteenth century and was no more than a historical memory by the twentieth, may seem pointlessly anachronistic. But the perverse tactics of Maurras and Lasserre were precisely to keep Romanticism alive, as an issue of burning topicality, for those who still needed to be convinced of the cultural barbarism in which France had lived since the Revolution. 'Romantic' ceased to be a historical or critical term; like 'democrat' or 'Jew' it became a term of abuse. It meant 'dissolute' or 'barbaric' or 'soft' (*mou*).[27] The Romantic, like the revolutionary, was an agent of decomposition. This last word, first used by Maurras in *La Revue encyclopédique* in 1898,[28] reverberates throughout his writings. Any writer whose works could be construed as favouring the rights of the individual against those of the community, encouraged social decomposition. So did the writer who, like the Romantic artist, presented the obscure, anarchic forces in Man as things to be brought into the light of day and cultivated for their precious uniqueness instead of suppressing and condemning them for their potential corrosion of a stable society.

These ideas were very much in the air, in traditionalist circles, around the start of Mauriac's career as a writer. His literary greats were Racine and Pascal, his most treasured period in French literary history the classical and 'Catholic' seventeenth century, the age of Bossuet, of Fénelon and of Port-Royal. However, he was also an avid reader, in his youth, of Chateaubriand and the Romantic poets.[29] But when, in his own early poetry, he draws upon the theme of Romantic *ennui*, he does so in a critical way. In a poem called 'L'Écolier', he writes of the school-boy of the title:

Pourquoi pleurer?—Il ne sait pas. Il veut pleurer
Comme René, dont il connaît les grandes plaintes.[30]

And Vincent Hiéron, Servet's lieutenant in *L'Enfant chargé de chaînes*, makes the same diagnosis of his friend Jean-Paul's state of mind: 'Ah! je le connais, ton mal (. . .) C'est le mal du siècle, le mal de René! Jusqu'à quand ce vieux débris romantique nous va-t-il encombrer?'[31] Jean-Paul himself, to his obvious credit in the eyes of the narrator, smiles at his own 'romantisme désuet'.[32]

The Romantic love of melancholy is a recurrent theme in Mauriac's articles and essays of the same period. Like all forms of love in his work, it is seen as akin to sexual love: René, he comments, clings to *ennui* as if to a dearly loved woman.[33] And like sexual love, it is a moral weakness. Fromentin's hero Dominique is stronger than other characters in Romantic fiction, he argues, because he fights against the ravages of the *mal du siècle*. And his ally in this struggle is the memory of the homeland:

Ses yeux se tournent vers les horizons voilés du pays natal.
Et le vieux jardin lui est un refuge, où à chaque tournant de
l'allée il rencontrera l'enfant rêveur qu'il fut jadis. Courageusement il va fonder un foyer.[34]

Here, aided by the comforting Barrèsian image of the landscape of his birth, Dominique embraces, like St.-Phlin, the institutions of marriage and family. That Jean-Paul, similarly moved by the memories of home and childhood, takes the same step—marriage to his cousin—suggests not only that Fromentin's novel is one source of Mauriac's, but also that *L'Enfant* (especially when one recalls also its presentation of the naïveties of Amour et Foi rhetoric) can be seen as a conscious contri-bution to the anti-romantic, socially conservative literature of its day. Its optimistic presentation of marriage and of the beneficial memories of home are, of course, untypical of Mauriac's work. His own mar-riage, imminent as he wrote the book, may partly explain this.

The theme of Romanticism then disappeared from Mauriac's writings for a number of years. It re-emerged, albeit in a more subtle way, in his literary essays of the 1920s. In *Le Roman*, for example, he asks whether the creative writer of the twentieth century can still accept the classical concept of a universal human nature. Should the novelist not concern himself with highlighting the most individual aspects of his characters, which make each one different from his fellows? If he does not do so, he argues, he must fail in his aim of reproducing the complexities of life. The traditional French novelist, indeed, was guilty of such a failure, in that he imposed too artificial an order on his characters, shaped them as neatly and as archaically as the gardens of Versailles.[35] By contrast, the novels of Dostoyevsky seemed to him to succeed in capturing the multi-faceted nature of individuals, their disconcerting, illogical, unpredictable behaviour. This lesson must be learned by French novelists. But—and here Mauriac takes a characteristic step backwards from his own radical proposition —the traditional French qualities of form and clarity must not be lost. The solution lies in a blend of Russian complexity and French order. The novelist must portray coherently the incoherence of human nature, create form in the presentation of the formless, yet always respect the essentially shifting and fluid character of his subject.

What is striking about Mauriac's attitude here is that in stressing the need to emphasise the individual differences in men he echoes the arguments of Romantic artists of a century earlier against the generalising principles of Classicism. But what of his ultimate insistence on order? Is this a purely aesthetic concept, or does it have its roots in profound non-literary sources, linking it to 'order' in a moral or even social sense?

The truth is that, in the novelist who was holding forth with such apparent confidence on the problems of his craft, the moral and social conscience was very much in conflict with the literary vocation. This is best illustrated by means of a comparison between *Le Roman* and a slightly earlier essay, devoted to moral issues, called *Le Jeune homme*. For in the latter Mauriac criticises the moral subversion of individuals who are discovering the very same truths in real life that, in *Le Roman*, he urges novelists to portray through their characters: the unreality of absolute categories of emotion, the irreducibility of individuals to a moral norm, the partial redundancy of earlier concepts of character. What dangerous lovers they are, he says, these young men to whom love, hate, desire and indifference are mere labels to mark the ebb and flow within them of their base instincts. What a previous age called love now seems as remote from real life, he goes

on, using the same image as in *Le Roman* but with diametrically
opposite implications, as the gardens of Versailles are from nature.[36]
To the artist in Mauriac, revolt against the imposition of a strict order
on fictional characters was necessary and constructive; to the moralist
in him, the same revolt, carried out on the plane of real life, was
positively alarming. For to deny the validity of a norm to which all
men could approximate could lead to the rejection of the rigorous
moral and religious code in conformity with which all men, in the
view of the Christian, should live. To marvel at the uniqueness of
each man's incoherent network of desires and emotions was to invite
men to become admiring spectators of their own inner labyrinth,
instead of urging them to be their own judges, cultivating the best in
themselves and rejecting the worst. He already saw, in the post-war
generation, the tendency to deny nothing of the self, to worship
impulse. The originators of this worrying trend ('ce fleuve trouble'),
he writes in *Le Jeune homme*, are Rimbaud, Dostoyevsky, Freud, Gide
and Proust.[37] Yet, of these five moral subversives, four are highly
praised by Mauriac, on literary grounds, in other writings.[38]

It is clear that by the late 1920s the opposing claims of art and
morality had locked Mauriac inextricably in self-conflict. How to
reconcile the exploration of Man with the possibly harmful results of
that exploration in the minds of readers? Perhaps the call to 'order'
in *Le Roman* represented an unconscious imposition of limits on his
own inventiveness, designed to discipline the terrifying products of
the imagination. Whereas Rimbaud, in his *Lettre du voyant*, had
insisted that the artist retain the formlessness of his originally formless
material—'Si ce qu'il rapporte de *là-bas* a forme, il donne forme; si
c'est informe, il donne de l'informe'—Mauriac's inclination was to
shape that material, so that its effect on the reader was not to reveal
the terrifying chaos in and around men but to offer him an aesthetic
structure which might conceivably hint at a superior order encom-
passing and eventually explaining the apparent incoherence of life.
He was always to associate the onslaught on traditional form with
moral subversion; behind the revolt of the Surrealists he saw, quite
literally, a supernatural force of evil, and in the work of the *nouveaux
romanciers* he was to detect a process of dehumanisation.[39] Like
Maurras, he was ultimately concerned, at least when he spoke with
his moralist's voice, with the impact of literature on its audience more
than on its inherent aesthetic qualities. He associated artistic discipline
with moral integrity, literary anarchy with moral laxity. And, to

return to an area where a direct comparison with Maurras can again be drawn, one finds Mauriac, in 1924, applying these same moral criteria to Maurras' hated Romanticism:

> Il existe un rapport certain entre la discipline intérieure et la perfection poétique; et ce que beaucoup haïssent sous le nom de romantisme, c'est le péché: le péché se trahit dans l'enflure, dans l'égarement, dans le désordre des images, dans le mépris du verbe, dans l'abus des épithètes. Le romantisme est le péché qui s'ignore: Charles Baudelaire domine son siècle parce que, chez lui, le péché se connaît.[40]

Maurras himself characterised Romantic style in equally coruscating terms and saw it, similarly, as symptomatic of a more general disorder. Two years before the publication of the text of Mauriac's that has just been quoted, he had written: 'La langue outragée, le rythme torturé, ce royaume des mots où la subversion engendrait l'ataxie faisaient penser aux subversions nées d'autres sources.'[41] His diagnosis, to be sure, was not identical to Mauriac's. To the agnostic Maurras, the Romantic was not the accomplice of sin, but of national weakness, through his encouragement of personal and supra-national values rather than wholly French ones. But that he and Mauriac should express a common opposition to Romanticism and to a literature of indiscipline is further eloquent testimony to certain fatal affinities between Catholic reflexes and conservative social attitudes. Maurras himself wrote in the wake not only of Bonald and de Maistre but also of Bossuet; and even in the last years of his life, as he worked on his final books in a prison library, he saw in both Old and New Testaments the confirmation of the rightness of his doctrine: that what he called 'social hygiene'—respect for hierarchical order—stems from the Christian code as shaped and civilised by the Church of Rome.[42] So the social reactionary and the Christian moralist could easily concur in their choice of enemies. The anarchist refusing to attune his nature to community values and the man spurning the moral one-ness prescribed by Mauriac in Le Jeune homme and elsewhere, could well be one and the same.

This latter point is worth exploring in greater depth, despite its apparent remoteness from the field of politics, because it is a central factor in Mauriac's ambiguity on all of these inter-related planes, the political one included, during his great creative years. Like all Christian thinkers, Mauriac, in his essays, stresses choice, the selection of what is morally good within the personality and the rejection of

contrary impulses. Christ, he writes in *Paroles catholiques*, acts like a
magnet on the personality, drawing the good elements into one
direction, creating a harmonious unity out of Man's multiplicity.[43]
The tendency of modern men not to choose, but to accept themselves
as chaotic, multi-dimensional beings, which he describes in *Le Jeune
homme*, runs counter to this process. The great enemy of Christianity
is the rejection of commitment in the name of a sincerity in whose
light all that is human is worthy.[44] Every reader of twentieth-century
French literature will know that Mauriac was not alluding to an
abstraction here, but to an adversary who lived and breathed and was
wont to write disturbing books: André Gide. Gide, above all others,
encouraged—or was seen as doing so by those who read his books
superficially—the free development of the multiple facets of the self.
His influence was deplored by Mauriac as being contrary to the
integrity which Christianity demands. In *La Vie et la mort d'un poète*
he censures the vogue of gratuitous action created by the success of
Les Caves du Vatican—action which by definition is out of line with
the conception of the personality as an organic whole.[45] Similar
criticism is expressed in *Paroles catholiques*[46] and implied throughout
Le Jeune homme. The effect of Mauriac's opposition to Gidism was to
bring him closer than he had been for some years to Barrès. Gide and
Barrès had long been rival attractions for him, each a purveyor in
ultimately opposed ways of a cult of self. This rivalry now resolved
itself into a choice between the autonomous self of Gide and the self-
guided-by-tradition of Barrès. Before the war, Mauriac had inclined
towards the model of Gidean *disponibilité*.[47] But in 1932, Gide's irritation with Barrès' supposed suppression of instinct, expressed in the
Nouvelle Revue Française, spurred Mauriac to Barrès' defence. He
stressed the constant effort of the man to surpass himself. 'Barrès a
passé sa vie', he wrote, 'à s'accorder. Gide, au contraire, s'établit
dans le désaccord.'[48] The death of Barrès had prevented him from
reaching the logical end of this process of harmonisation, which
would have been the acceptance of Christianity; for, to Mauriac, inner
harmony and discord were yardsticks of greater or lesser proximity to
Christ. To Barrès himself, of course, inner harmony was above all a
state of being that was propitious to the doing of great national deeds.
He places into the mouth of Sturel an analysis of Napoleon's superiority to his contemporaries Byron and Chateaubriand that rests on
his possession of inner unity.[49] And in the same novel, Roemerspacher's
realisation of 'notre besoin d'harmonie' is presented as the first step in

his eventual participation in national renewal.[50] So once again, the
Catholic values of Mauriac and the nationalist values of Barrès reveal
that they have a common grounding: this time, in personal stability
and discipline.

It emerges that the impression which Mauriac's novels give of his
moral and social position—defence of the individual against collective,
family attitudes—is an incomplete one. A close reading of his essays
in the context of traditionalist thought shows very clearly that his
stance on this issue was an ambivalent one. He was driven by fear of
the potentially harmful influences of his work to seek security in an
inner order which, while we have not yet established that it extended
to the social and political spheres, created a mistrust of indiscipline and
non-conformity that drew him temperamentally nearer to the ideolo-
gists of social order.

(iii)   Thérèse and Jean-Jacques

To confront the author of Le Jeune homme with the novelist who
wrote Thérèse Desqueyroux is to reveal even more starkly the gulf
between the moralist and the artist, each of whom called himself
François Mauriac. The contrast corresponds exactly to that between
Le Jeune homme and Le Roman, for while Thérèse represents the realisation of some of the artistic ambitions expressed in the latter essay—
the encapsulation in coherent literary form of the mystery and un-
fathomability of human nature—it also presents with acute ambiguity
some of the arguments pursued boldly and positively in the former.
In Le Jeune homme, as has been described, Mauriac opposes Gidism in
his view of the moral self as a persona we must create by an effort of
will out of the disparate urges within us. Self-creation, in this sense,
is a moral law. 'Pour dominer,' he writes, 'il s'agit d'être; mais nous
ne sommes pas: nous nous créons.'[52] In the novel, Thérèse echoes these
very words in her reply to Jean Azévédo's statement that we owe it to
ourselves to respond to the inner desires of our authentic being. 'Être
soi-même?' she asks. 'Mais nous ne sommes que dans la mesure où nous
nous créons.'[52] Does Thérèse speak here with the voice of Mauriac the
Christian essayist? Apparently so. But Mauriac the novelist intervenes
at once to diminish the impact of Thérèse's high-sounding words by
suggesting they are mere school-room platitudes. 'J'eus même recours
à des souvenirs de lectures morales qu'on nous faisait au lycée,' he
makes his heroine reflect as she recalls her retort to Azévédo. Or is
the reader invited to criticise Thérèse here for expressing such

fine moral precepts so half-heartedly, for not attacking the ideas of Azévédo more forcefully? Might Mauriac be making his own position clear when, in his essay *Souffrances du chrétien*, written the following year, he elaborates on this theme of self-creation? 'La personne morale existe,' he writes, '(. . .) que nous créons nous-même en nous. Mais les déchets qui ne servent pas à cette création continuent de vivre et de nous empoisonner.'[53] Is this, indeed, an indirect comment on Thérèse? Has her moral formation resulted in 'left-over' instincts which influence her actions, and is the poisoning of her husband a symbol of the poisoning of the true moral self to which Mauriac alludes here?

Clearly, the novel itself does not permit such fanciful interpretations, however desperately one tries to sustain them in the aim of making Mauriac seem a consistent moral thinker. The whole economy of the novel is shaped to point in the opposite direction, to suggest the strange nobility of Thérèse as a creature more sensitive, more honest, more redeemable in God's eyes than any of those around her, a victim and not a criminal, the nature of whose 'crime' postulates her potential elevation to saintliness as a 'sainte Locuste'.[54] Her actions are inexplicable to herself and to Mauriac. They defy understanding and thus prohibit condemnation, even in the name of Christian morality. Mauriac had reached a stage in his development as an artist at which the complexities of individuals seemed so great that they could not be circumscribed within any *a priori* morality, the Catholic moral code included. Self-creation may be a proper notion for a Christian essayist to propose, but in the crucible of Mauriac's fiction, in a Jansenist universe from which free will seems absent and self-direction impossible, this concept melts into mere words, into 'des souvenirs de lectures morales'.

What of the ideological adversary, Azévédo? He, in truth, is a disconcerting character, not easy to interpret. He represents submission to impulse, search for sensation, self-liberation. These are urges that initially stimulate Thérèse and which interest, aesthetically, the writer of *Le Roman*. But they are at the same time the impulses against which *Le Jeune homme* warns and which can be summarised in a word: Gidism. Azévédo expresses the preoccupations which run through Gide's writings, but they are stripped of the irony which is the vehicle of Gide's moral caution, and thus they embody that vulgarisation and distortion of Gide's ideas that was prevalent in the post-war generation. So Jean, like Thérèse, is a pointer to both of the directions in

which Mauriac faced: both to the exhilaration and to the irresponsi-
bility of individualism. And again, as in the case of the vague principles of Thérèse, Mauriac presents Jean's ideas and then dismisses them,
through Thérèse's mouth, as mere echoes of yesterday's reading. Not
sure of his own assessment of the values and dangers of individual
liberty, he equalises the opposing sides in the debate by presenting
each in turn as a possible victor and then dissociating his heroine from
it. A kind of uneasy truce is achieved between moral conservatism and
anarchy which, although it is propitious to the equilibrium of the
novel and allows the character of Thérèse to over-ride and ultimately
eclipse both too simple extremes, illustrates once more the unresolved
dilemmas of the author.

These divisions culminated in the profound moral crisis in
Mauriac's life, which erupted in 1928 and lasted for some two years. A
full account of this crisis would take us far beyond the limits of this
present study. It has been described, but not yet exhaustively, by
several students of Mauriac's career. No critic, however, has considered the relationship of this turbulent period to the evolution of
Mauriac's social outlook; but such is the complex inter-action of moral,
literary and social factors in his writings that such a question must
necessarily be raised here. To what extent Mauriac's work as a novelist
was affected by the crisis is a controversial issue. It is known that he
contemplated abandoning his career, only to go on writing but with a
more consciously orthodox Catholic outlook, which resulted, some
say, in a diminution of his creative powers. This is not the place to
debate this last issue. What concerns us is whether the adoption of his
post-crisis role as a virtual spokesman for his faith brought him yet
nearer to the traditionalist social and political views of many fellow
Catholics.

This question can be pursued by comparing certain aspects of
Thérèse Desqueyroux, which, rich novel that it is, holds still more
material relevant to this study, with a work written immediately after
the crisis: namely, his essay on Rousseau. As it appears in Volume 8 of
the collected works, as part of the collection called *Mes grands hommes*,
this essay poses certain problems of interpretation. The two parts into
which it is divided seem to have little to do with each other as far as
critical intention is concerned. The first part is a piece of polemic
against Rousseau, the second much less heated and less hostile to its
subject. The difference in approach reflects the fact that the two parts
were originally written as two separate prefaces, the first to the *Con-*

fessions (which contains much material likely to scandalise the Catholic moralist) and the second to the *Rêveries*, both written in 1929 for an edition of Rousseau's works and then brought together, somewhat casually if thriftily, in 1930, as one essay in *Trois grands hommes devant Dieu*. Each part can and should be read independently of the other, and each relates to *Thérèse Desqueyroux*, but in almost diametrically opposite ways. In the second part, commenting on Rousseau's insistence that his actions do not serve as a good guide to his essential character, Mauriac agrees. 'Il est trop vrai', he says, 'que nos actes ne nous ressemblent pas toujours, et c'est pourquoi tout jugement porté sur autrui est téméraire.'[55] This is the voice of the novelist, the voice raised in defence of Thérèse against a world all too eager to judge her entire worth on the basis of one single action. But in Part One, Mauriac takes exactly the same point and presents it quite differently. 'Rien ne nous ressemble moins que nos propres actes', he says, 'c'est cela que d'abord nous avons appris de lui. Rousseau traite ses crimes comme il a traité ses enfants: il ne les reconnaît pas.'[56] The second sentence transforms the first by casting an ironic light upon it. No longer does Mauriac express agreement with Rousseau's view, but sees it simply as a convenient plea that the notorious abandonment of his children should not be taken as evidence of total moral turpitude. Mauriac's attitude here is one of intransigent censure, and it leads him not only to refute, in advance, the second part of his own essay, but also to reject the principle on which he had based his own plea for understanding on behalf of Thérèse. 'Il ne reconnaît pas ses crimes,' he says disapprovingly of Rousseau, and invites our censure of the man. 'Je ne connais pas mes crimes,' he makes Thérèse say, soliciting our forgiveness of her.[57]

This verbal echo is startling, and it raises the question of the possible association in Mauriac's mind between his fictional heroine and his (perhaps equally fictitious) idea of Rousseau. There is strong evidence to indicate that such an association existed right from the time of his initial conception of the character and of the novel. Thérèse first saw the light of day in an original draft of the book, of which there remains only an embryonic fragment called *Conscience, instinct divin*, a title which derives from a well-known passage in Rousseau's *Profession de foi du vicaire savoyard*. In this passage, Rousseau describes conscience as an immortal and celestial inner voice, the guide of Man in the search for how best to use his God-given freedom; it is the infallible judge of good and evil, and to possess it elevates Man above the animal kingdom and makes him correspond more closely to God's image.[58] What might be objectionable here, in Catholic eyes, is that, while the sentiments expressed may sound admirably pious, the infallibility of judgment accorded to the individual conscience would make Man such an effective independent judge of his actions as to render both the Church and Grace quite superfluous. Rousseau's view of conscience can be seen from this angle, whether this is fair to him or not, as an essentially secular concept, and this is how Mauriac presents it in the essay: as an example of a Christian concept squeezed dry of true Christianity and pressed into the service of the Gospel according to Jean-Jacques:

> Et c'est seulement après s'être assuré qu'elle ne rendrait plus
> que des oracles favorables à sa passion qu'il a installé cette
> conscience avilie sur le trône même de Dieu, qu'il l'a adorée,
> qu'il lui a adressé des prières: 'Conscience, instinct divin'.[59]

Whether, three years earlier, Mauriac had intended as ironic the title of his first draft of the Thérèse story, and with it the whole presentation of the character of the woman who, conceived unlike the later Thérèse as a Christian, writes to her priest a would-be confession in which she usurps his priestly judgment in advance by declaring herself innocent by her own light, the short first version is too undeveloped for us to say. But the possibility of irony here should make the reader look closely at the use of the word 'conscience' in the final version of the novel itself. 'Sa conscience,' proudly say the teachers in the godless state *lycée* which Thérèse attended as a girl—'sa conscience est son unique et suffisante lumière.'[60] Her conscience, sole and self-sufficient, seeking no support from prayer or priestly mediation, does not operate on a spiritual or even moral level. It is a rational mechanism, and not a very efficient one, by which she surveys, without full understanding, the material reality of the events leading to the poisoning of her husband, but it has none of the moral self-questioning, the fear of transgressing divine law, that one would associate with Christian conscience. This totally unspiritual way of looking at her life informs Thérèse's whole approach to her investigation of her actions and motives, and places her in the lineage of that Rousseauist dechristianisation of moral analysis which Mauriac attacks in the essay, makes her initially prone to intellectual seduction by Azévédo, himself not only an embodiment of vulgarised Gidism but also a child of Rousseau by virtue of his doctrine of 'être soi-même'—the slogan, Mauriac says in the essay,[61] of all of Rousseau's modern descendents. Yet in spite of all this, Thérèse is forgiven by the novelist, writing in a genre which engenders compassion and understanding. There is no such pardon for Rousseau in the eyes of the moral essayist, however. Thérèse's confessional urge may be, after all, the sign of some obscure religious instinct, but that of Rousseau is motivated by callow self-justification. Rousseau's strategy is twofold. The first step is to blame all of his faults on society, to make it the scapegoat. The second is to defy men to say that they are less blameworthy than he: Mauriac quotes what he calls 'la ridicule prière du Pharisien qui sert d'exode aux *Confessions*: "Être éternel, rassemble autour de moi l'immense foule de mes semblables, (. . .) et puis qu'un seul te dise, s'il l'ose: je fus meilleur que cet homme-là" '.[62] But here, yet again, Mauriac reveals his own tortuous contradictions, for just a few years previously, in a prefatory note to *Le Fleuve de feu*, designed to ward off *bien-pensant* protests against so troubling a novel but ultimately more provocative than soothing, he had used a similar argument: if any reader doubted that it were possible for a good Catholic girl to fall as low as the novel's heroine, Gisèle, let him just look within his own corrupt soul. But now Mauriac had changed his whole angle of vision. The mote in Gisèle's eye had become the beam in Jean-Jacques'.[63]

The crisis had turned Mauriac, at least in the short term, into a sterner moralist than before. But that his new intransigence should take the form of an attack on such a controversial social and political figure as Rousseau is of great significance. It is the final piece in the jigsaw, completing a picture of the fatal overlap of moral ideas with social ones. For Rousseau is a litmus test of reaction. He is the fourth 'R' in Maurras' canon of hate, following Reformation, Revolution, Romanticism; the principal originator, indeed, of the last two and a living *résumé* of the spirit of all three. He is the villain of the piece in Maurras' *Révolution et Romantisme*: coming from Calvinist Geneva, where 'decomposition' was rife, spurred on by a doting old woman (Madame de Warens, not embellished by Maurras' chronic anti-feminism), he had wallowed in his private filth as social parasite and kept man, part criminal, part savage, part lunatic, before emerging on the public stage of Paris, the capital of a still great monarchy and model of all that was civilised. 'C'est ce bien magnifique,' says Maurras solemnly, 'qu'il tourna en calamité.'[64] Because of Rousseau, all that had stood the test of time—'tout ce qui était *fait*'—was undone: art, science, institutions, all corrupted or discarded in favour of pure, untouched individual nature. The individual, regardless of his merits, was elevated to new heights just because he was an individual. The hated egalitarian and democratic processes had spread everywhere, into literature, religion and politics. Such, says Maurras, was 'la qualité dissolue et dissolvante de l'impulsion donnée par Rousseau'.[65]

Maurras' assassination of the man, the fairness or unfairness of which need not concern us here, is on classic counter-revolutionary lines. It followed Lasserre's onslaught, the gist of which is resumed in the title of the first part of his book on Romanticism: 'La Ruine de l'individu (Jean-Jacques Rousseau)'. As for Barrès, one-time Third Republican deputy and no counter-revolutionary, his view was characteristically more nuanced. Rousseau, like Napoleon, was a multivalent symbol of national energy, his imagination 'un des grands ressorts de la vie européenne depuis plus de cent ans'.[66] But Barrès refused to give his allegiance in certain key areas. In a grandiloquent address to the Chamber of Deputies in 1912 he declared his refusal to participate in the celebration of Rousseau's bicentenary. Rousseau, he said, was responsible for branding society as unnatural, and had set the individual against it. In his educational theory, he had sought to remove the child from the beneficial influences of family and race. He had taught that society was artificial and that the family itself was held together by mere convention. This Rousseau Barrès could not honour.[67]

In view of this solid front of traditionalist opinion, it can be seen that Mauriac's criticism of Rousseau, couched in moral terms but involving the social in its defence of the community which Rousseau allegedly sought to blame for his own wrongs, was a further inportant step in his gradual movement towards the camp of order. Not necessarily influenced directly by the writings of Maurras or Barrès, he had nevertheless come to share certain of their attitudes in the years leading to and immediately following the crisis: their mistrust of the individual's anti-social nature, their opposition to the erosion of institutions, notably the family. Fear of his own subversive role, as a novelist, in this erosion now led him, perhaps not fully consciously, to repudiate many crucial aspects of his former outlook. His essay on Rousseau is a kind of anti-*Thérèse*. It is, manifestly, an ineffectual riposte to his fine novel. It was one thing to take a stern moral stand in the cool climate of a literary essay, quite another to do so in the more complex and dialectical world of art in which feelings and instinct can prevail and where, as Mauriac argues in *Le Romancier et ses personnages*, characters can escape the novelist's conscious control. Only through another novel, as impressive artistically as *Thérèse*, could he fully convince his public that he was not the arch-enemy of the family after all. The moralist in him had made his position clear, but Mauriac the novelist had yet to cede his ground.

(iv) *From knot of vipers to sacred family*

Mauriac the novelist had one more anathema to hurl at the family, perhaps the most ferocious of all. *Le Nœud de vipères* is a story of salvation. But it is also the story of the central character's solitude within a family whose members for the most part look eagerly ahead to his death and plot how best to ensure their inheritance. It is an indictment of the subordination of emotional and spiritual values to material ones, and it turns on the fact that Louis, father of the family and apparently, at the outset, the most materially minded of them all, reveals his true Christian sense in the end, in contrast to the conventional Catholicism of his wife and children. The novel is structured so as to win the reader's sympathy for Louis. As death approaches, he becomes more tolerant of weakness, forgiving his wife, his children and ultimately himself. But the final sequence of the book, the exchange of letters after his death between his son and daughter, shows their refusal to believe in his change of heart. The family has not learned its lesson. It cannot rise to the love and generosity which ought to give the family its *raison d'être*. Like the Desqueyroux, it can only accept what is convenient and undisturbing.

The novel began to appear, in instalments, in January 1932. Before the year was out, there appeared the first part of Mauriac's next novel, *Le Mystère Frontenac*, which was to present an almost totally opposed picture of family stability, of fraternity healing the tensions between individual members of the family group. The events of the eleven months separating the appearances of the two books were of great personal moment to Mauriac and important also for the light they throw on this latest apparent change of direction in his outlook. His health, precarious since childhood, suddenly deteriorated. He underwent an operation for the removal of a throat tumour and for six months his survival was a matter of some doubt. It was then that the French Academy elected him, by 28 votes for to 3 against, to the seat left vacant by the death of Eugène Brieux. Mauriac liked to relate his discovery that the supposed imminence of his own death had guaranteed his place among the immortals. Just after his election, he fell ill again, and the initial six months of anxiety lengthened into a two-year struggle for health. Moved by the care and attention of his family during 1932, he decided he did not want to die leaving Le Nœud de vipères as his last statement on family life.[68] To the editor of Le Temps, he wrote what amounted to a retraction of all that the previous novel had implied: how could he have depicted so ferociously an institution which was capable of such unselfish sacrifice? His new novel would be more truthful, he promised, more in accordance with his own experience of family love.[69]

There is no doubt that Mauriac's long war with his critics had been accompanied by less publicised conflicts, caused by his family's reactions to his portrayal of alienated husbands, rebellious wives, tyrannical mothers and smothered sons. Inevitably, there were members of his family who read his novels not as artistic transpositions of experience but as a kind of real-life portrait gallery.[70] They would be hurt, and worried about the image of the Mauriac family made public through the novels. This anxiety was expressed, not in totally humorous vein, by Pierre Mauriac in an address to his brother at the Bordeaux Academy following the Nobel Prize award of 1952: 'Que n'a-t-on supposé, Monsieur, de votre famille, dont vous sembliez déterrer le nœud de vipères au grand jour de vos romans?'[71]

Mauriac's new novel was consciously aimed at assuaging such misgivings. 'Avec Le Mystère Frontenac,' he writes, with just a tinge of self-irony, 'je faisais amende honorable à la race.'[72] Among the many autobiographical echoes in the book, one of the most poignant, when one recalls the circumstances of its composition, is the illness of Yves Frontenac, during which he is lovingly cared for by his brother Jean-Louis. Such fraternal devotion is a far cry from Mauriac's previous studies of family relationships, and it points to the Frontenac 'mystery' of the novel's title: that mystical bond which joins one Frontenac to another and which is God's gift to the family:

> Le mystère Frontenac échappait à la destruction, car il était
> un rayon de l'amour éternel réfracté à travers une race.
> L'impossible union des époux, des frères et des fils serait
> consommée avant qu'il fût longtemps, et les derniers pins de
> Bourideys verraient passer—non plus à leurs pieds, dans l'allée
> qui va au gros chêne, mais très haut et très loin au-dessus de leurs
> cimes, le groupe éternellement serré de la mère et de ses cinq
> enfants.[73]

What is interesting here is that the moral and theological mechanism on which the previous novels depended is thrown into reverse
gear. The result is a virtual negative of the familiar situation. The
family, hitherto the depository of violent and sinful emotion, becomes
the source of Yves Frontenac's awareness of Man's potential goodness.
'Il croyait à la bonté,' we are told, 'à cause de sa mère et de Jean-
Louis.'[74] Above all, the great Jansenist structure of a family tree
through whose branches flows a poisoned sap is replaced by the idea
of inherited goodness and love. An important point of divergence is
now eliminated between Mauriac's earlier mistrustful view of the
family's moral heritage and the more optimistic Barrèsian concept of
race. Barrès himself, it is worth noting, talked of 'mysteries' in the
same sense as Mauriac does in his story of the Frontenacs. 'Eh!
Messieurs,' Barrès declared to his fellow deputies during his attack on
the memory of Rousseau,

> nous savons bien que la société n'est pas l'œuvre de la raison
> pure, que ce n'est pas un contrat qui est à son origine, mais des
> influences autrement mystérieuses et qui en dehors de toute
> raison individuelle, ont fondé et continuent de maintenir la
> famille, la société, tout l'ordre dans l'humanité.[75]

How aesthetically successful the novel is in imposing its thematic
superstructure of family order on the flesh and blood of its characters
is a matter of minor importance here. Martin Jarrett-Kerr finds it 'the
most totally successful of the novels',[76] but John Flower's closely
argued study of its contradictions, the vestiges of more familiar
Mauriac situations that shine through and are not wholly reconciled
with the book's overall intention, is more convincing.[77] For our purposes, it is sufficient to say that, provoked by illness or not, the writing
of a novel to honour the family name was a logical step in Mauriac's
gravitation in the post-crisis period towards a morally and socially
conservative position. Le Mystère Frontenac is to Le Nœud de vipères
what the essay on Rousseau is to Thérèse: a refutation. That the two
refuted works stand so much higher in the scale of literary values than
the two which seek to refute them—for most critics identify Thérèse
and Le Nœud de vipères as Mauriac's greatest achievements—is an
ironic testimony to the fact that he was at his best as a writer when
semi-conscious remonstration urged him on, and less impressive as an
'écrivain à thèse', overtly trying to make a statement.

The view of the family in Le Mystère Frontenac was not a definitive
one. It is not the case that Mauriac never again cast doubt on the

family's values and authority, as *Les Anges noirs*, *Les Chemins de la mer* and his plays amply illustrate. His inspiration as a novelist was dependent on his experience, in childhood and adolescence, of the tensions between members of the family. If he wished to go on writing at all, he had to keep on playing the role of an Asmodée, lifting off the roofs of provincial houses and peering at the dramas within. There was always a conflict, which caused him lifelong heart-searching, between this need and his increasingly tender view of family relationships. What *Le Mystère Frontenac* represents is a moment when his qualms temporarily dominated him, and when he felt obliged, as he says, to make amends.

(v) *Mauriac's conservatism*

The relevance to social and political issues of this study of Mauriac's presentation of the family has depended on the importance accorded to the family in traditionalist social thought, both for its own sake as a disciplining force and as a model of social hierarchy ('Pourquoi juger la vie d'un pays', asks Bainville, 'd'après d'autres règles que celles d'une famille?'[78]). It is time to broaden the discussion and ask further questions about the social significance of Mauriac's novels. To what extent, for example, can he be seen as a commentator on social class or on the distribution of wealth and power in society? Can his scathing portraits of families be taken to signify the rejection of his own social class? Patently, the families in his novels are middle class families, and wealthy ones at that, their fortunes made in wine or timber. But there is a sense in which their social class is incidental to what Mauriac is saying. He did not choose the social milieu of his novels. They are set in middle class homes because to a novelist so dependent on the creation of atmosphere and the sense of place, only in settings familiar to him since childhood could he infuse into his work the feeling of 'being there'.[79] He writes of middle class people because he knows them. What interests him about them is not, primarily, what separates them from other classes, but rather the essential and universal characteristics of human beings which they embody. They are representatives of sinful, materialistic, uncharitable human nature. Their social class is secondary to this. Mauriac argued this point unequivocally. He was astonished, he implies in *Les Maisons fugitives*, by the exaggerated reputation he had acquired as a critic of the *bourgeoisie*, and he declares that there is no deliberate or conscious element of anti-middle-class feeling in his work.[80] His fullest statement of his position occurs in an article called 'Le Perpétuel malentendu', and it is worth quoting at length:

> Exemple frappant de ce malentendu entre un écrivain et ses jeunes lecteurs qu'aucun contact personnel ne permet de dissiper. De ce que mes personnages les plus misérables appartiennent tous à la bourgeoisie moyenne, ces garçons en avaient conclu que je condamnais ma classe et que, plus ou moins consciemment, je frayais la route à la révolution sociale.

> Or, je n'ai jamais eu d'autre souci que de peindre des hommes et des femmes tels qu'ils me sont apparus dans le milieu où je suis né.

> S'il existe une vérité à laquelle j'ai toujours cru, c'est qu'aucune classe n'a le privilège de la vertu, ni d'ailleurs de la pourriture. Au vrai, ceux qui dénoncent avec horreur la pourriture bourgeoise, nous doutons qu'ils puissent croire sincèrement à ce monopole de la classe moyenne. Hélas! les barrières sociales n'ont rien à voir avec la corruption de la nature: c'est dans le mal que le communisme d'abord se manifeste. En dépit des inégalités de caste qui frappent à la surface, une nappe souterraine d'égoïsme et de férocité alimente impartialement toute la race des hommes.

> Né du peuple ouvrier ou paysan, ou dans la plus haute aristocratie, j'y eusse retrouvé, avec des différences qui n'auraient pas touché à l'essentiel, tous mes héros, toutes mes héroïnes; et je ne les eusse pas moins chéris.

> Car le malentendu se poursuit jusque-là; certains de mes jeunes lecteurs, parce qu'ils les haïssent eux-mêmes, ont cru que je haïssais mes personnages bourgeois. Il faut bien les détromper![81]

Mauriac wrote this in 1933, the year of *Le Mystère Frontenac*, and it might be suspected that it is a convenient disclaimer in view of his imminent election to the Academy. But looking back over his novels bears out his statement that he never made any naïve distinction between evil bourgeois and innocent worker or peasant. The peasant parents of Claude Favereau, in *La Chair et le sang*, have their own failings: a brutish refusal to understand their educated son, whom they lock in his room to prevent him from rushing to the help of his master's son, who consequently kills himself. In *Thérèse Desqueyroux*, the mud that splashes up from under the wheels of the workman's bicycle, driving the heroine back against the wall as she walks away from the law-courts, or the devouring eyes of her coachman, signify the world's hostility just as clearly as any element in her bourgeois milieu. Nor did Mauriac see the enslavement of individuals by family as limited to middle-class circles: in *L'Éducation des filles*, he describes the peasant women of the Landes laden like asses under their burdens while their men-folk march proudly ahead of them, unashamed in their domination. The acquisitive instinct, the love of money and property, popularly identified as a middle-class vice, is regarded by Mauriac as having its roots in a pagan materialism that has been inherited by men at all social levels. Louis' working-class mistress and illegitimate son, in *Le Nœud de vipères*, are no less rapacious in pursuit of his money than is his regular family. And even the victims of the family, including Thérèse, share the attachment to wealth and land of their torturers. Thérèse is no anti-capitalist, and neither was Mauriac. His complaint against those who amass riches is not that they leave other men poor; the poor man would leave them equally destitute, given the chance. It is that love of money is as redoubtable a rival of love of God as sex is (more redoubtable in the case of the mediocre characters). It stands in the way of salvation—a source of much more acute anguish to Mauriac, so uneasy where salvation is concerned, than any social injustice that might result.

To see Mauriac as a class traitor, on the grounds of his novels, is to make a serious misrepresentation of his work. Both Jean-Louis Bory and Jacques Laurent, writing in a special number of *La Parisienne* devoted to Mauriac (May 1956), try to draw parallels between some of his political opinions in the 1950s, which, to be sure, were not always popular with middle-class readers, and his allegedly anti-bourgeois novels. Such comparisons are tempting but facile; the facts provide no justification for them, and they merely divert attention from deeper, more significant common patterns between Mauriac's fictional and journalistic writings that will be discussed later in this book.

To the end of his life, Mauriac was to reiterate the acceptance of, and affection for, the middle classes which he announced in the 1930s. It is not the role of the Church, he declared in 1965, to instigate a redistribution of income. The Church recognises that there are rich and poor in spirit in all social classes, and harbours no prejudice against the *bourgeoisie*, knowing what true virtues and hidden sanctity reside in that branch of society.[82] And of the family, he wrote just before his death that this most ancient of institutions, now under more pressure than could ever have been imagined forty or fifty years earlier, must be defended. He recognised the role his own novels might have played in undermining its authority, but now, to Gide's cry: 'Familles, je vous hais!' he would respond: 'Famille, je te bénis.'[83]

Mauriac was a social conservative. He saw no need for any radical change in the social structure. The essential reforms are those that have to be achieved within men, in the privacy of individual hearts and minds, and no amount of institutional reorganisation can further this end. This he stated in 1932, in a polemical article directed, once more, against Gide. The old adversary, at that period, had espoused socialist faith in collective progress; to this, Mauriac opposed the individual's struggle to reach moral perfection. To Gide's declaration that religion and family were the worst enemies of progress, he retorted that inner progress could find no surer guarantors than family and religion: Gide's argument to the contrary, he went on, proved only that moral advancement and the collective progress dreamed of by the Left were not only different, but fundamentally in conflict the one with the other:

> Nous voyons clair maintenant. (. .) Progrès intérieur selon le Christ, progrès extérieur selon le marxisme, nous en revenons toujours aux deux cités dressées l'une contre l'autre jusqu'à la consommation des siècles. J'ai foi en la puissance de celle qui paraît la plus faible.[84]

And when a chastened Gide returned from the Soviet Union, disillusioned by the restoration of the family and the survival of the 'bourgeois' acquisitive habit which he had witnessed there, and sorrowfully admitting that men could never be reformed by external measures,[85] Mauriac must have permitted himself a satisfied if un-Christian 'told you so'.

The emphasis placed by Mauriac on the Christian basis of his opinions raises yet again the ever-recurring question: could he, as a Catholic, have taken any stand other than a conservative one? The obvious answer is that, as a free man, he could. Despite the concordance of views on so many issues between Catholics and traditionalist social thinkers, no Catholic need consider himself any more bound to extreme conservatism than any other man. During the 1930s there were many Catholics who were determined to destroy what the liberal Dominican newspaper *Sept* called the old confusions between Christianity and certain political positions.[86] Within the Church hierarchy the liberal Cardinal Liénart and, in Catholic journalism, men like Francisque Gay and Emmanuel Mounier were among the leaders in a movement towards a new open-ness in social and political matters, a new Ralliement. Rome encouraged this trend, a fact that its condemnation of the Action Française in 1926 seemed to underline; while the politician execrated by Maurras, that erstwhile separator of Church and State Aristide Briand, now found favour with many Catholics who detected, in his pacifism and internationalism, attitudes that Christians could and should adopt. Paradoxically, this new (and tragically short-lived) current within French Catholicism was the vindication of all that Marc Sangnier, denounced little more than twenty years previously, had stood for. And the man who had been in an ideal position to learn Sangnier's vital lesson—the separability of Catholicism from reaction—the man who was later to claim that he had never forgotten that lesson, preferred at this moment to support more orthodox attitudes.

From July 1932 onwards (a month after his apology for Le Nœud de vipères) Mauriac found a platform for his increasingly voluble political comment in L'Écho de Paris, a newspaper very sympathetic to the Action Française, and whose leading light was the ultra-conservative Général de Castelnau, head of the intransigent Fédération Nationale Catholique. Some of his contributions to the paper have been reprinted in the first volume of his Journal, such as the article 'La Petite flamme' of August 12th, 1933, which derided the left-wing, 'masonic' criticism of Catholic schools.[87] Another article mocks the trendy and insincere leftishness of certain financiers,[88] while another, 'L'Age de la réussite', comments on the fatal restrictions imposed on politicians by the circumstances of party and parliamentary institutions.[89] These are relatively anodine articles. More substantial is one which Mauriac apparently chose not to have reprinted in later collections, the article 'Propos sur la guerre et sur la paix', in which he allied himself with Général de Castelnau on the subject of patriotism. Castelnau, as radically anti-German as Barrès and Maurras, placed national honour above peace. He had been opposed by 'Christianus', a journalist of La Vie intellectuelle, who censured sabre-rattling nationalism in the name of Christian charity and made the distinction between true patriotism and integral nationalism: the latter, he said, was as excessive as the barbaric national-socialism across the Rhine. Mauriac intervened at this point to defend the nationalists. It was all too easy to attack patriotism, he declared, and he implied that Catholic nationalists were patriotic to a degree that men of the Left can never achieve.[90]

Thus he had by now completely reversed the position he had adopted just before the Great War, when, in his lecture on 'L'Idée de Patrie', he had criticised the excessive and anti-Christian nature of absolute nationalism and denied its monopoly of patriotic fervour.

So how close did Mauriac stand now to Maurras and the integral nationalists? Eugen Weber's opinion that he approved of much of what Maurras represented, though it is based on somewhat hearsay evidence—Pierre Mauriac's testimony to his brother's 'sympathy' for the Action Française, Mauriac's alleged sleepless nights after the papal condemnation of the movement in 1926, his presence at the funeral of the assassinated integral nationalist Marius Plateau[91]—seems a valid one in the light of the findings revealed in this present chapter. Yet Mauriac remained capable of independent thought. To portray him as merely an unavowed or reluctant Maurrassian is to do him less than justice. In particular, there was one chink of daylight between him and the reactionary Right, a gap between their respective positions which would broaden into a chasm from the late 1930s onwards: namely, Mauriac's total lack of anti-semitic prejudice. Hatred of the Jews had been a feature of Maurras' outlook ever since his political *début* at the time of Dreyfus. The Action Française was a product of the Affair, and the support it found in the Catholic *bourgeoisie* was due in no small measure to its exploitation, in the wake of Édouard Drumont, of that mixture of religious bigotry and commercial envy that made anti-semitism endemic there. Mauriac's family had been fiercely anti-Dreyfusard, with the exception of his uncle Louis, and the name of Dreyfus was made gruesomely familiar to him during his schooldays, at the height of the Affair, for 'dégrader Dreyfus' was the name which the boys of his Marist school gave to their version of the universal schoolboy game of divesting flies of their wings and drowning them in ink-wells.[92] He was conscious also of the anti-semitic propaganda and the vicious cartoons of the 'bonne presse'—especially the Catholic *Le Pèlerin*[93] and the Bordeaux monarchist paper *Le Nouvelliste*.[94] Many years later, he was to describe such piecemeal condemnation of the innocent Jewish officer as 'ce criminel détournement de la conscience catholique'.[95] He claimed, characteristically, that his eyes had been opened to this collective crime by Sangnier and the Sillon.[96] But the earliest reference to Dreyfus in Mauriac's writings is in the novel *Le Nœud de vipères*, in which anti-semitism is regarded by the hero Louis (based partly on Mauriac's uncle) as a particularly vicious example of the false Christianity around him. So during the very period in which Mauriac was signalling his adherence to the Right on so many questions, he also issued an important reminder that there were attitudes in that section of the political spectrum which he still loathed. The point Mauriac really makes by his retrospective Dreyfusism is that he still prized men above institutions. Despite the instinctively conservative attitudes that his milieu and education had fostered within him, and which the Sillon had been unable to eradicate; and despite the anxiety at the moral laxity of his age (and his fears of encouraging and sharing in it) which led him to seek stability in orthodox values, he did not believe that the establishment was always right. Justice to individuals had to be done. His deep Christian concern for his fellow man, uneasily co-existent with his often austere moralism, dictated that Mauriac would still support the underdog against the weight of collective opinion if his conscience told him his cause was just. In his abomination of the unjust and inhuman treatment meted out to Alfred Dreyfus there lay the germ of his Christian and humanitarian response to the persecuted people of Ethiopia, the Basques of Guernica, the Jews in Hitler's death-camps. Events were now about to bring to fruition, on the world plane, Mauriac's profound Christian charity and to sever his links with the traditionalist Right.

Part Two

MAURIAC'S SECOND CAREER

Chapter Three

NEW DIRECTIONS, 1933–1958

(i) *Away from the Right*

Mauriac's right-wing position depended to a large extent on an accordance of outlook with conservative or reactionary thinkers: fear of moral and social anarchy, desire for the security which strong government and rigorous social order are alleged to provide. These attitudes are real enough, and certainly no mere abstractions. But they belong to the plane of generality. Men had expressed them in virtually every period of French history since the initial revolution which, historically, had fostered such reaction. Maurras, their principal defender, was saying much the same things in 1935 as he had said in 1905; and Mauriac's views, up to the time of his entry into the French Academy, were also based on the same pre-war conceptions of society which inform his novels. The war itself, with the examples it seemed to offer of mismanagement by politicians, had strengthened such attitudes and the supposed bleeding of the middle classes by what Mauriac, as late as 1936, called the 'fiscalité meurtrière' of Republican governments[1] corroborated them further in the inter-war period. But even traditionalist thought has to adapt itself to the times, or restate its applicability to them in precise and actual terms. Mauriac's views, subordinate in any case to his involvement in his literary career during most of the period, had not yet had to face the challenge of cataclysmic events that would test their tenability to the utmost. When those events came, they swept along with them a man like Maurras, too inflexible to shift his ground. But they proved Mauriac to be a much less doctrinaire man, willing to redefine his social and political standpoint. His realisation that it was, and must be, redefinable, expressed in 1933, suggests that he was in the process of awaking to the realities of the age. 'Mais il est passionnant', he told readers of *L'Écho*

67

de Paris, who may not have thanked him for doing so, 'de vivre à une époque "qui bouge", lorsqu'on a, comme nous, passé sa jeunesse dans un temps où les positions semblaient prises une fois pour toutes.'[2]

The events of this period, a period 'in motion', to echo Mauriac's understatement, need no elucidation. To a Frenchman, they meant the existence abroad of conflicting ideologies and rival models of society and, at home, a corresponding polarisation of political positions between admirers of the Soviet system on the one hand and of the Fascist dictatorships on the other. To Catholics and conservatives, the ogre was Communism, so much so that the dictators were, at worst, lesser evils; at best, they were saviours, strong men showing the direction in which France herself should develop. The advent of Hitler to the German Chancellery in January, 1933, resulted in an amplification of those voices that had been urging, ever since the rise of Mussolini over a decade earlier, that France too should invoke its *meneur*, its own Duce or Führer to reverse the tide of socialism and restore national strength.

The failure of such a figure to emerge was the subject of one of Mauriac's by now regular fortnightly articles in *L'Écho de Paris*, called 'L'Homme qui ne vient pas', published on July 1st, 1933. Mauriac first exploits the absence of a great national chief in order to attack the parliamentary system. French institutions prevent the formation of such leaders, he says, and even when exceptional men do appear, their fate is linked to that of a party, and thus, in the notoriously unstable ministerial regime of the Third Republic, they never stay in power long enough to exert real and lasting influence. Individual talent is wasted, potentially inspiring men have their fires extinguished by the tepid waters of routine administration. Parliament is a 'panier de crabes', a kaleidoscope of interchangeable faces, unable to command the respect of the nation, particularly of the young. But having made this point, Mauriac strikes out in a different direction. He argues that, despite the institutional obstacles to his appearance, if the French really wanted a Hitlerian overlord they would create one. Their unwillingness to do so is not a sign of weakness but of strength, a recognition by Frenchmen that their country's traditions are civilised ones, not to be maintained or restored by daubing their faces and crouching on all fours like the barbaric beasts they fear and mistakenly think they respect. The answer for France, says Mauriac with a patrician distaste for Hitler's intellectual and social pedigree, is not to call down a house-painter from his ladder and exchange his brushes for the

reins of government. Is Hitler's Germany so admirable? Does not its
social order simply mask confusion and violence? Is she not Medusa
rather than Minerva? 'Croirons-nous que nous sommes inférieurs,'
he goes on,

> parce qu'aucun aventurier n'a encore su capter, en France, les
> forces ténébreuses? Parce que chez nous toutes les familles
> spirituelles [a reference to Jews as well as Christians] ne sont
> pas prêts à s'anéantir sous le regard de la Tête aux cheveux de
> serpents?[3]

Thus Mauriac denounced Hitler from the outset, and stated his
belief that the greatest bastion against a Hitlerian regime in France lay
less in the actions of government than in the innate civilisation of the
French. But in 1933, such a comforting view was hardly likely to
bolster the cause of the Western democracies. Mauriac's failure to
envisage an institutional expression of collective good taste, his refusal
to recognise that parliamentary democracy, accused by him of pre-
venting the flowering of individual leadership, is more properly a
safeguard against the abuse of personal power, prevent him from pre-
scribing any effective solution to potential demagoguery. He was not
yet speaking with the voice of a responsible political commentator.
Although he had realised where the greatest external danger to France
lay, his anti-parliamentarianism in a period when extremism was
rampant and a *putsch* looked possible, could only contribute to a
weakening of internal security.

The same ambiguity marks several of his subsequent articles in
L'Écho de Paris, in which both the regime and its French Fascist adversaries are scathingly censured. His article on the Stavisky scandal, in
many ways a novelist's article in its preoccupation with the sentimental motives behind Stavisky's financial dealings, ends with an
exposure of the collusion between Republican politicians and crooked
financiers or 'pleasure-merchants'.[4] Yet his article a few months previously on 'L'Idée de Nation' warned these same politicians against
one of their greatest enemies: former men of the Left, former socialist
internationalists and one-time despisers of the patriotic concept of the
Nation. These men were so impressed, he said, by what Hitler and
Mussolini had achieved by appealing to national pride that they now
sought to harness patriotism to a new doctrine of French national-
socialism. He identified Marcel Déat as a man particularly anxious to
exploit this possibility, to 'reprendre au fascisme ce que le fascisme a
appris de nous: le culte de la nation une et indivisible'.[5] He does not

mention Maurras here: his targets are men of even more ferocious extremism; and he sees Fascism, in any case, as having its roots in the revolutionary tradition rather than the reactionary one—'le jacobin préfigure le nazi', he affirms.[6] But he was clearly beginning to realise that the national idea, for which Maurras had campaigned for some forty years, could so easily be corrupted, with disastrous results.

So far Mauriac had not set his sails against the Right, but only against its Hitlerite fringe. His interpretation of the confused and violent events of February 6th, 1934, when the right-wing Leagues made their abortive, ill-concerted attack on the Palais-Bourbon, was in keeping with that of the conservative and nationalist press. To him, this had been a legitimate expression by 'the people' of their discontent with the government. For, he argued, the Left's concept of the people —'(le) prolétariat ouvrier'—was limited and false. The middle classes, too, were a part of the people, and a sorely tested part. 'Les chômeurs et demi-chômeurs en veston sont innombrables.' The bourgeois down on his luck, the bankrupt business-man whom Mauriac was to portray so sympathetically in his novel Les Chemins de la mer, was as much a victim of the economic incompetence of governments as the underpaid worker. And the lesson he drew from this was that a reconciliation was now required between the old Right's demand for strong government and the moderate Left's cries for social reform.[7]

This article thus shows a tolerance towards the Leagues, a willingness to understand and sympathise with the forces that drove them, which conflicts sharply with Mauriac's retrospective view of the period expressed in the preface to his Mémoires politiques, where he makes little distinction between the majority of the Leagues and the violent Cagoule.[8] On the first anniversary of le 6 février he declared his compassion for the demonstrators killed in that night's street-fighting: they had died in vain, he said, for the government had done nothing in response to their claims.[9] But tolerant towards the Right or not, the concessions he favoured in the direction of social justice for the working class were of too pink a hue for the editorial committee of L'Écho de Paris. His contribution to the paper ended in April 1934. 'Le très catholique Écho de Paris', remarked Emmanuel Mounier, 'a trouvé M. François Mauriac (. . .) un peu trop communiste pour le goût de ses lecteurs.'[10]

In truth, of course, Mauriac was immeasurably distant from the Left. His attitude to the advent of the Popular Front, formed in response to the right-wing activism of February 6th, and achieving electoral success in May 1936, was one of near panic as he contemplated economic destruction for the middle class. Listening to an electoral broadcast by the Communist leader Maurice Thorez a week before the first ballot, he was aghast at the promised squeeze of the *bourgeoisie*. He complained that his own family, not one of the notorious 'two hundred', had already been ruined by the fall in the value of their investments. A vote for the Left, a vote for the Communists, was unthinkable.[11] And of Thorez' famous offer of friendship to Catholics, Mauriac not only suspected an electoral manœuvre, but also reminded the readers of *Le Figaro*, to which stoutly conservative paper he had now removed his column, that Communists, like Nazis, were the enemies of all spirituality, and that a Christian, conscious of his individual duty to choose between good and evil, could never subscribe to a totalitarian society in which he would be required to absorb his own moral conscience in that of the mass.[12]

In none of these declarations did Mauriac dissociate himself from the mainstream of right-wing opinion. His denunciation of Hitler did not involve this, for the old anti-Germanism of the French nationalists was still strong enough to prevent Hitler from being more than an ambivalent figure, although admirable on some counts, notably in his estimation of Jews and Communists. The truly exciting foreign personality, to Maurras and his followers, was Mussolini, leader of a Latin and Catholic nation, whose doctrines owed a great deal to the ideologies of the Action Française itself. Mauriac's attitude to Mussolini, therefore, was crucial to his relationship with the Right in his own land, and the test of it came when the Duce's armies invaded Ethiopia in the autumn of 1935.

The spring of that year found Mauriac endorsing a view of Germany and Italy that was common in Maurrassian circles: the German race was incompatible with the French, committed as it was to a disastrous war in which its own terrible losses would not matter to it as long as the democracies suffered even more; and he welcomed with great relief, therefore, the *rapprochement* with Italy that the Laval–Mussolini pact seemed to signify.[13] And when the invasion came, he did not support the liberal Catholics Bidault, Mounier and Pierre-Henri Simon or the former Maurrassian Jacques Maritain in their backing of Britain's call for League of Nations sanctions. His one comment, though, was a telling one. It took the form of a criticism of a cartoon, drawn by Sennep for the right-wing paper *Candide*, showing the Emperor of Ethiopia perched on top of a palm-tree with two

monkeys, clutching a copy of *L'Humanité*. This drawing encapsulated
all that the pro-Mussolini faction, notably Maurras and Général de
Castelnau, had been arguing: that it was not worth breaking the pact
with Italy, even risking a European war, for the sake of a few savages
whose political principles, if they had any, probably leaned in the
wrong direction in any case. Mauriac remarked: 'C'est très drôle et il
faudrait rire. Mais par habitude professionnelle je me mets à la place
des gens.' He asked what the response would be to such humour
among the black populations of France's African territories, many of
whom were the sons of men buried somewhere between the Channel
and the Vosges. And were not these 'savages' in Ethiopia, waiting to
be killed by the weapons of civilised men, deserving, for all their
primitive way of life, of Christian compassion instead of the mindless
sneers of journalists? Though Mauriac spoke here from strong moral
indignation, he was still hesitant to enter into political debate with
Mussolini's supporters: perhaps the invasion was justified, and Mussolini had 'de la grandeur' in any case. But his position was made clear
nevertheless: no amount of political argument could justify the shed-
ding of innocent blood. The gulf between this conviction and the
Politique d'abord! slogan of the Action Française could not have been
wider.[14]

Mauriac, to whom support for the Popular Front was still out of
the question, but who was dissociating himself more and more from
right-wing opinion, was fast running out of potential political allies.
Between the two extremes there lay an important third force to which
he now gravitated: the liberal Catholics, represented for some years by
papers like *L'Aube*, but who now had a new vehicle in the publication
Sept, established in 1934 under the auspices of the Pope—a sign of the
current but short-lasting official blessing of the old Sangnierist line of
Christian democracy. What led Mauriac to contribute to *Sept*, and to
sever his associations with the conservative wing of Catholicism, was
the Spanish Civil War. That this was a great turning-point in his life,
and the launching of his second career as political journalist, he explained to Madeleine Chapsal in 1960:

> J'ai commencé à me détacher de la fiction au moment de la
> guerre d'Espagne. (. . .) Je vivais jusque-là dans une espèce de
> rêve, de monde fictif, et la guerre d'Espagne a réveillé le garçon
> sillonniste que j'étais à vingt ans. (. . .) L'horreur du monde réel
> m'a chassé de la fiction.[15]

Spain, in the early summer of 1936, presented to Frenchmen

almost a mirror image of their own troubled and divided land. In both countries Popular Front governments had come to power, and the rebellion of the Spanish Right, embodied in the person of Franco, foreshadowed to many the civil war that they felt was bound to erupt in France as well. Spain was France as she might be six, nine, twelve months hence. Thus political attitudes in France towards the opposing sides in Spain were polarised in exactly the same way as they were in the face of domestic tensions. The Socialist and Radical supporters of Blum's government, as well as the Communists who had helped him win power, were totally sympathetic to Spain's legally constituted republican regime, while the French Right, including the large majority of Catholics, were equally committed to the revolt led by Franco, seen as a crusade to restore order and Christian values to a country that had slid into ungodly anarchy. Thus the events in Spain actually seemed capable of accelerating the coming of France's own holocaust, especially when, in July 1936, the Madrid government telegrammed to Blum requesting aid in the form of arms and aeroplanes.

Mauriac's immediate reaction to the possibility of French intervention across the Pyrenees is interesting, for it contradicts his many later versions of his unequivocally anti-Right stand. Within a week of the request from Madrid, he declared in no uncertain terms his opposition to intervention on the side of the Frente Popular. In an article in *Le Figaro* on July 25th, which, unlike his later anti-Franco articles, he did not see fit to have republished, he warned Blum what such intervention would mean:

> Il faut que le président du Conseil le sache: nous sommes ici quelques-uns à essayer de remonter le courant de haine qui emporte les Français depuis l'avènement du Front populaire, nous nous sommes efforcés à la modération. Dans une atmosphère de guerre civile, nous avons voulu 'raison garder'.

> Mais s'il était prouvé que nos maîtres collaborent activement au massacre dans la Péninsule, alors nous saurions que la France est gouvernée non par des hommes d'Etat, mais par des chefs de bande, soumis aux ordres de ce qu'il faut bien appeler l'Internationale de la Haine. (. . .)

> Et je crois être l'interprète d'une foule immense (. . .) en criant à M. Léon Blum, qui brûle d'intervenir, qui peut-être est déjà intervenu dans ce massacre: 'Faites attention, nous ne vous pardonnerons jamais ce crime.'[16]

So his comments, many years later, on the failure of Blum to give effective help to the Spanish Republic are of dubious honesty.[17] His first response was like that of most other Catholics, already suspicious of their left-wing masters and determined not to be led by them into military involvement. Writing in 1938, he explained his standpoint of July 1936, describing it as that of a man of the Right and saying that it was dictated by his horror at the atrocities against political prisoners in Barcelona and elsewhere, perpetrated by government supporters.[18] And what decided his definitive detachment from majority Catholic opinion was his no less intense horror at the atrocities carried out by pro-Franco forces in the city of Badajoz in mid-August. The murderers of Barcelona had set the original example of mass killing, he insisted, but those of Badajoz had been quick to follow it; and what was worse was that the latter represented the so-called Christian side in the conflict.[19] 'Ce qui fixa notre attitude', he explained later, 'ce fut la prétention des généraux espagnols de mener une guerre sainte, une croisade, d'être les soldats du Christ.'[20] His wrath was directed especially against Franco himself. 'Ce chef catholique qui se dit soldat du Christ'[21] was a man that Mauriac was to execrate right up to his death. 'Franco', he told his son Claude, 'a fait que des millions d'Espagnols voient dans le Christ l'Ennemi n° I.'[22] This view was also expressed in Mauriac's preface to Victor Montserrat's book *Le Drame d'un peuple inconnu*, in which he asked how many centuries would have to elapse before the Spanish Church, or even the Church of Rome in general, would wash itself clean of the fatal association with the massacres of Guernica and Durango, and destroy the link forged in the minds of the survivors between the crucified Christ and the avenging Franco.[23]

This bitter regret at the possibly irreparable damage done by Franco to the Catholic religion in Spain was at the centre of Mauriac's view of the war from late 1936 onwards. Hugh Thomas overstates his political position when he describes him as being 'in favour of the Republic'.[24] Rather did Mauriac regard all the ideologies represented in the conflict, whether of Left or Right, Republican or Franquist, as mere excuses for killing. 'C'est toujours le même sang qui continue d'être versé au nom des mêmes Dieux: Patrie, Peuple, Ordre, Liberté, Démocratie.'[25] Thus, when André Malraux returned from Spain in February 1937 and spoke in support of the Republic, Mauriac opposed his attempt to make political capital out of the Right's atrocities: that could only exacerbate and prolong the war, not help to end it.[26] And it was to the government authorities in Spain, not to their adversaries, that Mauriac, together with Gide, Duhamel and Roger Martin du Gard, addressed a telegram demanding an assurance of respect for political prisoners.[27] If Mauriac appeared to be particularly revolted by right-wing atrocities, it was because, paradoxically, of a certain prejudice on his part: murder was less surprising when committed by men who had rejected God. When done in the name of Christianity, it was odious, and he reacted accordingly.

So moral and religious issues took precedence in Mauriac's mind over purely political ones. Nothing illustrates this more clearly than his particular concern for the plight of the Basques, who, as supporters of the government that had given them their long-awaited autonomy shortly before the war, had been brutally attacked by Franco and by the planes of Hitler's Condor Legion. Immediately after the destruction of Guernica, Mauriac signed a pro-Basque manifesto (together with Maritain, Mounier, Charles du Bos and Gabriel Marcel) and joined Maritain's committee in their defence, eventually becoming its president.[28] In the pages of *Sept*, he urged French Catholics to rally to the cause of this ancient Christian people, whose only help had come from 'les ennemis mortels de l'Église' (defined by him as Communists and Anglicans). The spectacle of Catholic killing Catholic in the name of Catholicism was one that he could not tolerate: the union of Catholics against violence must now be proclaimed.[29]

This appeal went unheeded. Mauriac, with Mounier, Maritain and, most spectacularly of all, Georges Bernanos, remained in the minority among French Catholics. To Claudel and to the Catholics of the Action Française, Franco's campaign was a just, even a holy one; and that the Church hierarchy itself shared this view was illustrated by the suppression of *Sept* by Rome in late 1937. 'Nous aurons passé notre vie, depuis la condamnation du Sillon,' remarked Mauriac many years later, 'à voir se rallumer cette flamme souffreteuse sur laquelle Rome ne se lassait pas de souffler pour l'éteindre.'[30] But no sooner had *Sept* ceased to exist than had Mauriac found another platform in the liberal Catholic weekly *Le Temps présent*. Here he collaborated with leading Christian democrat writers like Stanislas Fumet, Joseph Folliet and Georges Hourdin, writing articles and giving speeches in Paris and various provincial centres. Mauriac's courage in thus openly defying the strictures of his Church, with which his relationship since his crisis had been easier than before, is undeniable. Bernanos, who had hitherto been so cool towards his fellow Catholic novelist, acknowledged this by sending Mauriac a copy of *Les Grands cimetières sous la lune*, that most memorable of all protests, by a Frenchman, against the barbarian in Spain. It was inscribed as follows:

Ce livre ne peut passer que par la brèche que vous avez ouverte si courageusement et si noblement. Puissiez-vous ne pas le trouver trop indigne de vous! De toute mon admiration et de tout mon coeur.[31]

So the two leading Catholic novelists of the period now found themselves on the same side in French involvement in Spain—a situation that would hardly have been imaginable in those days a generation earlier when one had been a member of the Sillon and the other a Maurrassian Camelot du roi. Now, both inspired by the same compassion that informed their work as imaginative writers, they expressed their opposition, not just to the majority of their co-religionaries, but also to the man and the movement that still served as a focal point for Catholic opinion in France: Maurras and the Action Française. The intellectual links between the French integral nationalists and the Spanish Right were strong. Among the most important groups committed to Franco's cause was that centred on the *Acción Española* newspaper, its doctrines consciously modelled on those of its French forerunner. And to Maurras' men, Franco's troops—not rebels, but 'nationalists' —were, hopefully, precursors of those legions who might soon overthrow France's Popular Front and with it the whole Republican and democratic edifice. To Mauriac's deploring of the attack on Guernica by Nationalist forces and their allies, they opposed their version: that the town had been set alight by the Russians for their own propaganda purposes.[32]

This most irrevocable of all polarisations between Mauriac's position and that of the man whose ideas he had long found seductive was manifested not just in newsprint, but also in the arena of the French Academy. On his election to this august body in 1933, Mauriac had been, by his own admission, politically naïve. He saw his role in a purely literary light, remote from political considerations.[33] But that he was unlikely to find himself seated next to a friend of Léon Blum was something he must have known from the start. The Academy, a centre of Orleanism for much of the nineteenth century and staunchly anti-Dreyfusard at the beginning of the twentieth, included in its ranks in 1933 such *colossi* of the Catholic, royalist and military establishment as Bourget, Bordeaux, Pétain and Weygand. And a little reflection might have led Mauriac to conclude that his own election, engineered by Henri Bordeaux, could not have been hindered by his position, at that time, on the right side of the political fence. His knowledge of the conservative outlook, as individuals, of his fellow immortals was one thing, however; quite another was his discovery of the subterranean world of intrigue into which his election initiated him; a world where a writer's political views were not merely one potentially relevant factor in his chances of electoral success, but the essential factor, overriding literary merit; and where, increasingly, such skilful stage-managers as Pierre Benoît were plotting the access to the influential platform of the Academy of their friends on the Right or extreme Right. Membership of the Academy was a positive educative force in Mauriac's political life, and had an effect on his movement away from the Right in those years just before the war that it would be hard to over-estimate. His enlightenment began as early as March 1935, when a triple election saw the arrival under the Coupole of Jacques Bainville, André Bellessort and Claude Farrère. All three were friendly, in only slightly different degrees, to the Action Française: Bainville as the foremost nationalist historian of the day, Bellessort as a regular lecturer on literature and drama in the Institut d'Action Française, and Farrère as president of the 'patriotic' Association des Écrivains Combattants. Mauriac recorded no comment as far as the first two men were concerned: he no doubt found Bainville's election unexceptionable on literary grounds alone. What shocked him was the success of Farrère against the rival candidature of a writer of much greater stature: no less than Paul Claudel. This election, 'la plus scandaleuse', says Mauriac, 'qui se soit jamais perpétrée quai Conti',[34] was due to the execration of Claudel, despite his unflagging defence of right-wing positions from Dreyfus to Spain, for his service as a diplomat of the Republic.[35] Mauriac's 'shame'[36] that France's literary establishment was capable of such baseness led him, he says, to open his ears and to understand that the goal of the pro-Right lobby in the Academy was the election of Maurras himself.[37]

Maurras was elected in June 1938, and Mauriac was one of the twelve academicians to vote against him.[38] His motives in doing so, however, were probably no more pure—or, at least, no more purely literary—than those of the twenty who voted in favour; for viewed solely as a writer, Maurras outshone his opponent, the poet Fernand Gregh. Mauriac's opposition was really a gesture of political protest, with the concerns of Catholicism again uppermost in his mind. To make Maurras' candidature respectable in Catholic eyes, a reconciliation had had to be effected between the Action Française and Rome, and to this task Georges Goyau, the permanent secretary of the Academy, and André Chaumeix had applied themselves despite the fact that both had been for years the victims of insults emanating from the pages of Maurras' journal.[39] The spectacle of Goyau, whom Mauriac remembered with affection as a regular guest speaker in the Réunion des Étudiants, now bending over backwards to ensure Maurras' acceptability, offended him deeply.[40] It was another example of the tragic compromise of French Catholics with a man who was fundamentally opposed to the bases of their faith. Mauriac, at one stage in danger of a similar entanglement with Maurrassian values, now had a clear understanding of where he himself stood: against the ideologies of the Action Française, based as they were on a solely institutional concept of civilisation, and for a political creed which, although its precise details were still vague in his mind, must have true Christian and humanitarian compassion at its heart.

(ii) *War and Occupation*

Mauriac once described the French Academy of the late 1930s as a liquid in which Vichy France was already suspended.[41] The prestigious figure of Marshal Pétain stood at the centre of its anti-Republican majority, whose commitment to the Maurrassian doctrines that were to form the ideological basis of Pétain's state was unquestionable. There were even academicians like Louis Bertrand who, less marked than Maurras by ancient anti-German passions, now openly proclaimed support for Hitler. Such sentiments were echoed more and more loudly in the wider context of the country at large, where exasperation at the continuation in power of the Popular Front and the conviction that Bolshevism had replaced the old German foe as the main threat to France were giving rise to a Fascist extremism in comparison with which Maurras and his men, notwithstanding their calls for violent action against Blum and others, looked more and more tepidly conservative.

To Mauriac, Hitler was the primary danger, and in Nazi anti-semitism he saw a moral evil overriding even questions of national security. From 1937, he had been a member, along with Maritain, of the committee of the review *La Juste parole*, formed to combat anti-Jewish propaganda—its ironic 'correction' of the title of Drumont's paper *La Libre parole* is obvious. At the time of the *Anschluss*, in 1938, he took a leading part in organising a reception centre for Austrian refugees, mostly Jews.[42] Like the atrocities committed against the Basques in Spain, the German aggression in Austria was, in Mauriac's eyes, an onslaught on a Catholic people, and he regretted that France had not gone to Austria's aid.[43] Such bold views were less in evidence, however, at the time of the Munich talks later that year. Mauriac declared his joy at the apparent success of the Munich meeting from the French and British point of view, seeing the concessions to Hitler as likely to lessen the danger of war. He even wondered whether the Western diplomats had not succeeded, after all, in touching hard German hearts.[44] But precisely two weeks later, he was taking the opposite view:

> Et peut-être sauverons-nous encore une fois la Paix, en donnant 'quelque chose' au Minotaure—en lui jetant quoi dans la gueule? Que nous reste-t-il, après l'Autriche, après la Tchécoslovaquie? Que détenons-nous encore qui soit à la mesure de la grande faim? (...)
>
> Le 'premier' anglais ou le 'premier' français entreprendra derechef, en avril ou en mai, le pèlerinage de Berchtesgaden pour consulter l'oracle. Et nous connaissons la réponse de l'oracle. Elle sera brève et claire: 'Coupez-vous un bras!'[45]

It may be that Mauriac's initial reaction to Munich was influenced by the optimism of his colleagues of Le Temps présent, for they, especially Folliet, expressed similar opinions. Or perhaps, as he later suggested, he was driven to wishful thinking, due to his fear for the lives of his sons if war broke out.[46] In any event, his enthusiasm for the Western spokesmen in October 1938 must raise doubts about his fairness, and also his historical judgment, when, years later, he utterly denounced the policy of Chamberlain, to the extent of declaring Britain responsible for the war.[47]

When France fell, in the early summer of 1940, Mauriac's diagnosis of the national collapse differed only from that which de Gaulle was to make in that it was couched in deeper spiritual terms. To de Gaulle, the catastrophic military blunder of foreseeing a static war instead of one that would be won by mobilised strike forces was the proof of a lack of national will.[48] To Mauriac, this national unpreparedness was itself symptomatic of moral decay. The disaster was due not just to material causes, not merely to the inferiority of France's air-force and artillery, but to a weakness of a spiritual nature.[49] His attitude was shared by many people in various sectors of French opinion. As Jacques Duquesne says,

> Quasi spontanément, (. .) l'idée a surgi que la France était
> coupable, qu'elle a été pour cette raison abandonnée par la
> Providence et battue, que cette défaite est donc méritée, et même
> qu'elle peut être salutaire.[50]

This willingness to beat the collective breast was certainly salutary to
Pétain, who was quick to encourage it, agreeing that 'l'esprit de
jouissance' was the cause of the disaster,[51] and thus diverting guilt
from the defeatist attitudes which he himself had helped to encourage.

As widespread as this tendency to mass confession was a reluctance
to denounce Pétain, even among those who opposed either full collaboration or even a truce of any sort. This was true, in the early years
of the Occupation, even of Resistance papers like *Combat*, *Liberté* and
Les Petites ailes, and it was true of the large majority of Catholics, and
especially of the Church hierarchy, whose support for Pétain in 1940
and 1941 went beyond the Church's traditional policy of supporting
the established government. Pétain was the saviour who had delivered
France both from the most brutal excesses of Nazi domination and
from potential anarchy in the hour of defeat. Some bishops decreed
that it was morally wrong not to support him, and such incidents as
the refusal of the sacraments to Mounier because of his anti-Pétain
sentiments strongly suggested that not to be a Pétainist was tantamount
to being in a state of sin.[52]

Mauriac was on the side of the majority in his expression of
admiration for Pétain. He reacted to the latter's radio broadcast of
June 25th, 1940, as follows:

> Les paroles du maréchal Pétain, le soir du 25 juin, rendaient
> un son presque intemporel: ce n'était pas un homme qui nous
> parlait, mais du plus profond de notre histoire, nous entendions
> monter l'appel de la grande nation humiliée. (. . .) Une voix
> brisée par la douleur et par les années nous apportait le reproche
> du héros dont le sacrifice, à cause de notre défaite, a été rendu
> inutile.[53]

But as the last sentence of this passage makes clear, Mauriac dissociated
himself from the extreme view that France, under Pétain, was entering
on a great new era. Defeat was defeat, and nothing could reduce the
humiliation of that, not even the old soldier's heroic assumption of
national destiny. Mauriac's sympathy was with Pétain, the hero of
Verdun, the man now forced into a tragic situation by what he saw
as his duty to the nation. Besides which, as he explained later, he
wondered—in common with a great many people,[54] including

Hitler[55]—whether Pétain might not be playing a double hand, through a secret alliance with his former *protégé* de Gaulle.[56]

So when Mauriac's enemies try to make capital out of his admiration for the Head of the Vichy state, they do so by a deliberate distortion of the facts. 'En 1940', writes Pol Vandromme, 'il préférait Pétain à de Gaulle.'[57] This view appears to have originated from an article by Mauriac called 'La Vérité', which appeared in *Le Figaro* on June 19th, 1940. This begins:

> Le 17 juin, après que le maréchal Pétain eut donné à son pays cette suprême preuve d'amour, les Français entendirent à la radio une voix qui leur assurait que jamais la France n'avait été si glorieuse. Hé bien non! il ne nous reste d'autre chance de salut que de ne plus jamais nous mentir à nous-mêmes.
>
> Reconnaissons que nous sommes au fond d'un abîme d'humiliation. (. . .)[58]

According to Jean Nocher, who seems to have initiated this particular myth, the broadcast against which Mauriac reacted so unequivocally was none other than de Gaulle's famous appeal from London, his call to the French people to rally to the cause of the Resistance and of the Free French in exile. Thus, says Nocher, Mauriac's claim to have been an early supporter of de Gaulle is a lie.[59] But Nocher's case is easily demolished. Firstly, the three crucial opening words of the article—'le 17 juin'—make it impossible that Mauriac could have been alluding to a speech that was broadcast on June 18th; secondly, nowhere did de Gaulle, in that celebrated speech, say that France had never been so glorious as she was in the defeat of 1940; and thirdly, even had he wished to do so, he would hardly have been accorded the facility of Vichy radio: Mauriac is clearly referring, not to a B.B.C. broadcast but to one on the national network. All of this is plain to any fairminded reader of the text in question, but when, in the 1960s, his opponents resurrected the legend to question the consistency of his Gaullist allegiance, Mauriac was obliged to defend himself.[60] Even that did not stop the attempted exploitation of the issue, for an anonymous writer in *Carrefour* quoted the article yet again as late as 1968, deliberately omitting the words 'le 17 juin', in a blatantly dishonest attempt to discredit Mauriac's stand of more than a generation earlier.[61]

In fact, Mauriac emerges in a very honourable light as a consistent opponent of truce and collaboration. In April 1940, he declared himself against an armistice, and said that France must fight on, in spite of the odds, and in the hope of a lasting peace afterwards.[62] He was soon recognised by collaborators as a resolute opponent. On November 11th, 1940, Jean-Luc Dulac wrote an article in *Le Cri du peuple* called 'M. Mauriac, le tartuffe belliciste'. The collaborationist paper *Jeunesse* followed suit in January 1941, while in June of that year a lecture was given in the Théâtre des Ambassadeurs on 'Mauriac, agent de la désagrégation française'. This was attended by Jean Guéhenno, by Father Maydieu of *La Vie intellectuelle* and other Catholic intellectuals, who roundly booed the speaker.[63] Also Lucien Rebatet, in his book *Les Décombres*, found space amidst gross denigration of Bernanos and Maritain to describe Mauriac as 'une fielleuse hyène'.[64]

Mauriac later expressed his gratitude to these vicious men—gratitude because they helped him to take stock of where he now stood politically.[65] He must have been surprised, indeed, by the transformation in his outlook and reputation during the last few years. Had Pétain been empowered by a quirk of fate to set up a Vichy state or something like it a decade earlier, before Ethiopia and Spain and in circumstances unsullied by national military collapse, Mauriac would probably have given it his allegiance. So, indeed, would de Gaulle! To many Frenchmen, Vichy seemed the answer to an oft-repeated prayer, the prayer for deliverance from parliamentary government, anarchy and the threat of Communist insurrection. For Catholics especially, the Vichy interlude was a period of religious revival, of what Robert Paxton calls 'the closest church-state harmony since the 'moral order' regime of the Duc de Broglie and Marshal MacMahon in 1873–4'.[66] Several laws, dating back to the anti-clerical days of the turn of the century, were now repealed. Religious instruction was restored to state schools, to the approval of all who felt, with General Weygand, that 'la France (. . .) a été battue parce que ses gouvernements depuis un demi-siècle ont chassé Dieu de l'école'.[67] Church property, confiscated in 1905, was handed back. The Carthusian order, expelled years earlier, was welcomed back to its traditional Alpine fastnesses. Tighter divorce laws were instituted to secure the strength and authority of the family. The Vichy slogan *Travail, Famille, Patrie* was accepted as 'ours' on behalf of all Catholics by Cardinal Gerbier. And to those who liked their Catholicism to be accompanied by severity towards the alleged adversaries of the Church, the banning of 'clandestine' groups (that is, the freemasons) and the anti-Jewish laws of the later part of the war were not insignificant either. On a more ridiculous level, Paul Claudel composed a homage to Pétain, to be declaimed during the *entr'acte* of a performance of *L'Annonce faite à Marie* in the unlikely setting of the casino at Vichy.[68]

Mauriac could rejoice in none of this, for the religious revival, if that was what it was, was a triumph not for the spirit of the Church but for the institution, a victory for the Catholics of the Action Française. Vichy seemed a vindication of all that Maurras had preached for so long. Though he did not use the famous phrase 'a divine surprise' in the context in which he was alleged to have done—he was referring not to the establishment of Vichy but to Pétain's revelation of unsuspected political abilities—Vichy must have seemed to him an unexpected if not unsollicited gift from the gods. 'Ce qui se réalise', wrote the Maurrassian Paul Courcoural,

> (. . .) c'est la Contre-Révolution. Avec Charles Maurras et tous ses amis nous (. . .) saluons les premiers actes (de Vichy) avec une émotion, une fierté et une espérance qui s'expliquent par toute notre vie depuis cinquante ans dévouée à ces principes.
> (. . .) On ne fera donc plus, en France, que de l'action française.[69]

This 'action' included a denunciation by Pétain of the 'false notion of the natural equality of men': his promise to make the regime and the country 'a social hierarchy', 'hierarchised and authoritarian'; the forbidding of public service and of admission to the legal profession to *métèques* and their sons; the repeal of all naturalisations since 1927; the Charte du Travail inaugurating a corporatist order in place of the old boss-worker conflict; and the anti-masonic and anti-Jewish laws already mentioned. All of these were in keeping with Maurrassian ideology[70] and must finally have proved to Mauriac where Pétain and Vichy stood: partners in no secret pact with the Resistance, they were the vehicle by which the ideas of the man once admired, now execrated by Mauriac were coming to full if tardy fruition. And thus Mauriac was driven into opposition to the regime, and into the Resistance.

His first contact with the latter was in the autumn of 1941, when he was introduced by his friend, the novelist Jean Blanzat, to the group organised by Jean Paulhan and the left-wing writer Édith Thomas. This group, which met first at Blanzat's house and later at that of Édith Thomas, merged with another, larger one, the so-called Comité National des Écrivains, the meetings of which were attended by Sartre, Éluard, Queneau, Camus and others.[71] The Comité had been founded by a young writer and teacher called Jacques Decourdemanche, known as Jacques Decour, and its initial preoccupation was to found and publish its journal, for which a title was quickly chosen: *Les Lettres françaises*. Their programme was thrown into disarray, however, by the arrest and execution of Decour early in 1942. Even worse might have followed, for their security procedures left much to be desired: Mauriac himself unwittingly delivered evidence of Paulhan's participation to a disguised Gestapo agent,[72] and this situation, as well as others arising from a string of denunciations, was retrieved only by the activities of an anti-Nazi German officer, an old college friend of Paulhan (and also of the ambassador to Vichy, Otto Abetz).[73] It was to this officer, Gerhard Heller, that Mauriac dedicated the first edition of *La Pharisienne*, his only wartime novel. This sign of apparent friendship with the enemy caused a small stir at the time; in retrospect, it seems surprising only in that it might have led to suspicions, on the part of the Gestapo, of Heller's pro-French attitudes.

When, in September 1942, the first number of *Les Lettres françaises* appeared—a simple, four-page roneotyped edition—it included a declaration by Mauriac of his dedicated participation in the activities of the C.N.E.[74] And, as a member of this group, he was automatically associated with the larger association—one of the largest of all Resistance groups—to which it was affiliated: the Front National. This was the political wing of the military unit known as the Francs-Tireurs et Partisans. Although it drew its support from a wide spectrum and included such eminent Catholics as Bidault, the Front had been dominated by Communists since the latter joined the Resistance following the invasion of Russia in 1941. The C.N.E., too, gradually became a Communist-dominated group. In later years, Mauriac manifested some embarrassment at these wartime associations. He had not set out to join the Front National, he quite truthfully stated, but had become a member by accident: 'parce que mon réseau de résistance s'y était inféodé'.[75] Yet, in the context of the Occupation, there was nothing disreputable about membership of the Front. Certainly, as de Gaulle was to note in his war memoirs, the movement, 'd'aspect purement patriotique', aimed to exploit the situation and help lay the ground for an eventual seizure of power in France by the Communists; but de Gaulle also saw the Communists, for the moment, as the lesser of two evils, themselves to be exploited until the expulsion of the Germans from France was assured, and then to be met in a new confrontation.[76] Thus, to belong to the Front did not necessarily imply long-term Communist allegiance. De Gaulle's own cousin Henri Maillot joined it in Corsica, believing that doing so would in the end serve the interests of Gaullism.[77] In any case, according to Brian Crozier, 'those who joined the National Front usually belonged to some other Resistance organisation and were ignorant of party control over the Front'.[78] This was partly due to the nature, by necessity, of the group's clandestine operations, and partly due to its deliberate dilution of Communist ideology in order—for sinister reasons or not—to attract men of all political tendencies. 'Marxist–Leninist doctrine', writes Crozier, 'was swept out of sight, apparently forgotten. Instead, the party extolled the virtues, deeds and names of the French Revolution of 1789'.[79]

It is interesting to consider the influence of these associations on Mauriac's writings during the Occupation. His contribution to the literature of the Resistance was not a large one in terms of bulk. 1940, before he joined the C.N.E., had seen him contributing to Le Figaro and to Le Temps présent the occasional article lamenting his country's plight. He deplored, for instance, Britain's sinking of the French fleet at Mers-el-Kebir.[80] De Gaulle, though he strove manfully to see this latter tragedy from a British viewpoint,[81] wrote of Mauriac's articles that they brought tears to the eyes.[82] From the end of 1940, however, Mauriac was very silent. His novel La Pharisienne contained allusions to the Occupation that were so discreet as to be virtually unnoticeable;[83] and, otherwise, he had little desire to write. The winters of 1941 and 1942, spent at Malagar, with a German officer occupying an upstairs room, seemed one long, icy blackness, freezing literary and polemical initiative.[84]

When he did take up the pen again, in 1943, it was to reveal himself in an increasingly radical mood, determined to fight for a national future from which all of the old class and religious prejudices would be abolished, notably the prejudices for which the Action Française stood, and around which so many Catholics had tragically rallied. In his article 'La Foi en l'homme', published in Lausanne in 1943, he recalled the gloomy view of Man as predator that lies at the heart of Maurras' system, and he stressed the opposition of Christianity to such 'doctrines of death'. They were based on a scorn of Man, whereas the Christian message proclaims that even the worst elements in Man can be transformed and utilised towards his moral improvement. Such inner progress was possible for nations as well as individuals. To deny this, to deny that Man could avoid the destiny of Cain, was to reject the truth of the Redemption.[85]

Significantly, in a minor text of the same period, Mauriac looked back ruefully at his earlier attacks on that notorious disseminator of indulgent views of human nature, Rousseau, and declared that Rousseauist optimism was more attractive than the misanthropic doctrines of the Rousseau-haters in the Action Française. It was time to destroy the old reactionary myth that 'c'est la faute à Rousseau'. Rousseau was a writer to whom he himself owed a great deal, he said, and of whom he wished to detract his previous disparaging views, influenced as they had been by counter-revolutionary demonology.[86]

By 1943 there was close contact between the C.N.E. and the clandestine Éditions de Minuit. One important name was missing from the list of contributors to the Éditions, thought Jacques Debû-Bridel, by then one of the C.N.E.'s leaders: that of Mauriac. Through Blanzat's agency, he visited Mauriac, who read to him a text composed as early as 1940. 'Ce seraient les plus belles pages des Éditions de Minuit', writes Debû-Bridel.[87] The text was Le Cahier noir, and it was published soon afterwards under the pseudonym of Forez. It was a more obviously political text than the articles which preceded it, though it rested on the same notion of faith in Man's dignity and potential goodness. It records what Mauriac called his 'balbutiements de rage' in the face of the actions and pious declarations of Vichy. How ironic, he comments, that such traditionalist regimes only seem to flourish in France in the wake of military defeat, feeding on humiliation and on the protection of the enemy. And how enlightening that Pétain's desire to find scapegoats for the national disaster should lead him to pick on the Jews. He also indicts those ideologues who stand behind Pétain, the purveyors of 'realist' politics, champions of Politique d'abord! He identifies such men as standing in the lineage of Machiavelli in their exclusion of morality from politics, and sees them as allies, through their dehumanisation and despiritualisation of politics, of the totalitarian regimes which have covered Europe in blood. And, he goes on, every innocent victim of this merciless persecution, be he Christian or pagan, Communist or Jew, shares in the martyrdom of Christ. In opposing these modern Machiavellis, Mauriac echoes so unmistakably a passage from Le Mystère Frontenac as to make his use of an authorial pseudonym almost pointless. Yves Frontenac, sitting by an ant-hill and watching the ants devouring each other, had been struck by the revelation that human life need not be subject to such pitiless carnage: an act of love is sufficient to break the bloody chain. Here, in almost the same words, the lesson is transferred to the world stage and becomes a clear rejection of the Maurrassian view of human relationships:

Mais nous avons fait notre choix; nous parions contre
Machiavel. Nous sommes de ceux qui croient que l'homme
échappe à la loi de l'entre-dévorement, et non seulement qu'il y
échappe, mais que toute sa dignité tient dans la résistance qu'il
lui oppose de tout son cœur et de tout son esprit. Non, l'esprit
humain ne s'abuse pas sur sa destinée. Non, il ne se trompe pas en
protestant que la condition des termites et des fourmis ne l'éclaire
en rien sur la sienne. N'y aurait-il eu au cours des siècles, en un
bref intervalle du temps et de l'espace, qu'un seul mouvement de
charité, la chaîne sans fin des dévorants et des dévorés en eût été
à jamais rompue . . .[88]

So traditionalist values, according to Mauriac, had been corrupted by amoral cynicism. This view led him, for the first time, to
declare his adherence to the republican and even the revolutionary
traditions. 'Ceux qui m'insultent', he says, in reference to the Vichy
journalists (and also to those, even more ferocious, of the overtly
collaborationist Parisian press), 'sont aussi ceux qui crèvent de joie
parce que la République est morte (parce qu'ils croient qu'elle est
morte)'. Dead, too, or so the counter-revolutionary forces think, is
France's role as teacher and guardian of liberty, which Mauriac sums
up—in keeping with the Front National's exaltation of the men of the
Revolution—in Saint-Just's phrase: 'Le peuple français vote la liberté
du monde.'[89] Most guilty of the rejection of this facet of the national
vocation was the middle class, its values now safeguarded by Vichy's
corporate, moral order regime; and the victim was the proletariat, its
hopes recently raised by the coming of the Popular Front, but now
relegated to its customary role as Samson under the Philistines' whips.
Yet the working class, at least, has not participated in the great
national betrayal. 'Seule la classe ouvrière dans sa masse aura été fidèle',
says Mauriac, 'à la France profanée.'[90]

His only other important contribution to Resistance polemic was
his essay La Nation française a une âme, also written in 1943, and published in a fuller version following the Liberation. Less well known
than Le Cahier noir, it develops just as forcefully and perhaps with
greater analytical clarity the same thesis: the paradox of nationalists
who have sold out to the enemies of their nation while members of the
working class, supporters of parties that are internationalist and supra-
nationalist in spirit, have resisted those enemies in the true interests of
their fatherland. Two lessons, argues Mauriac, are to be drawn from
this reversal of political positions. The first is that the kind of authori-

tarian dogma perpetrated for so long by Maurras, by Bainville and in
Léon Daudet's daily 'paquet d'ordures', must never again be allowed
to contaminate the minds and hearts of the nation. Liberty must be
fought for, with force if necessary, and the old revolutionary slogan,
truncated by the 'timides républicains' of the Second Empire, must be
restored to its full and necessary form: *Liberté, Égalité, Fraternité OU
LA MORT*. And secondly, a new nationalism must replace the old: a
revolutionary patriotism based on the pride that the working class has
rediscovered in itself and in the country through the brotherhood of
the Resistance. 'Rien n'empêchera désormais les Français de tous les
partis,' he declared,' (. . .) de demeurer unis autour de cette idée de
nation. (. . .) L'esprit de '93 revit enfin.'[91]

This was heady stuff, and in truth Mauriac was at this moment
further to the Left than he had ever been. His assertion that true
patriotism was to be found in the proletariat was a repetition of what
he had said as a young man in 1912 (and refuted between the wars),
and that he should now return to such a view in his maturity was
probably due in some measure to the influence of the left-wing
Resistance militants with whom he was now in close contact. By
gradual stages, since the time of Ethiopia, he had progressed to a total
openness of mind, an admirable willingness to unite with men whom
he would earlier have regarded as enemies of his class, his faith and his
values. The experience of war and occupation had lifted from the eyes
the distorting filter through which he had instinctively surveyed men
of the Left during the period of the Popular Front. He now felt a
greater affinity with an anti-Vichy Communist than with a pro-Vichy
Catholic. The ground was now prepared for Mauriac, former man of
the Right, to emerge in the post-war period as an influential intellectual of the Left.

(iii) *The remaking of France*

Before the war, Mauriac's comments on political matters had been
relatively infrequent. They were also invariably hesitant, the work of
a man eager to admit his lack of credentials for venturing into a field
foreign to his talents. He could only bring to bear the artist's point of
view, he insisted; no doubt specialist political writers would find his
arguments inadequate.[92] The Liberation revealed a writer transformed. Both in the proportion of his writing devoted to the public
scene—he had now begun to contribute a regular column to *Le Figaro*
—and by the increasing confidence with which he expressed his

opinions, it was plain that Mauriac had embarked on nothing less than a second career: that of political journalist. For a while, in his enthusiasm for his new role, he played the part of a professional newspaper-man, attending press conferences and debates in the Assembly. Later, he would prefer to comment on the issues of the moment from a distance, above the *mêlée* of ordinary press-men, his articles taking shape in response to, or more usually in protest against, the views of other political commentators.

The writings with which he heralded the Liberation, the first of them (his celebrated homage to 'le premier des nôtres', Charles de Gaulle) courageously written from within still occupied territory— from his wife's property at Vémars (Seine-et-Oise), liberated a few days later than Paris itself—can be read, in the collection *Le Bâillon dénoué*, as a moving evocation of the complex moods of that late summer and autumn of 1944. They are marked by a wide range of tone. Again and again Mauriac writes with deep solemnity of those who have died, and of those who are still being killed, for the sake of France's and Europe's freedom. 'Quelle chose sans valeur', he laments as he looks back on German reprisals for the acts of the Resistance,

> est devenu un garçon de vingt ans, au bord d'une route! Les derniers Boches en auront fusillé par douzaines, chaque jour, sans presque y prêter d'attention . . (cinquante d'un seul coup, dans ma ville natale, dont vous, cher Jean Barraud. . .)[93]

He recalls also the horrors of a camp near Compiègne where French Jews were starved to death.[94] He laments the death in action of his friend, the writer and leading Stendhalian Jean Prévost.[95] This anguish, and his deep feeling for the French people as they shivered in their unheated homes during the desperate winter of 1944,[96] are leitmotivs in his writings of the time. But rising buoyantly above them is the sense that Frenchmen now have an opportunity greater than for years past to create a new France. In characteristic sexual and religious imagery, he describes France, so recently 'une nation violée et souillée', as 'une nation réveillée comme Lazare'.[97] Paris was free: the hated Swastika flag—'cette araignée gonflée de sang'[98]—no longer flew over the Place de la Concorde. Through the autumn of 1944, the rest of the country knew freedom as well. But France must not, in her joy, allow events to overtake her. She must work to sustain the unity created through the Resistance. The Fourth Republic must remember its origins as 'la fille des martyrs'.[99] Catholics and atheists, Communists and priests had fought and died together to achieve this freedom,[100] and the co-operation they had shown, the burying of ideological differences in the common cause, was a lesson not to be forgotten. Unity was necessary and also possible, given a willingness to recognise the common ground between the disparate elements in French society and to understand and accept the differences. The working class's role in the Resistance was such as to demand recognition in the concrete shape of social reforms, and the more privileged sections of society, far from combating this, must work for it, and pull down the curtain on an era where the rich were the occult masters of the state.[101] Co-operation with the proletariat in this venture would enlighten and rejuvenate the bourgeoisie, by the very fact of contact with the working masses, 'source de toute vie'.[102] 'Car nobles et bourgeois,' he insisted, 'paysans et ouvriers, vous êtes tous de même lignage, vous êtes tous des fils de France.'[103] Likewise, Christian and Marxist need no longer be mortal enemies. The rejection of Hitlerian and Maurrassian scorn of men in which they had shared had revealed the bond that could unite them. The socialist might prefer to see Man as the supreme being: the Christian saw Man as God's prime creation. On both sides was a respect for human values which promised a rapprochement: the extra, spiritual dimension in which the Catholic saw mankind need not stand in the way of this.[104]

Thus did Mauriac, quoting Saint-Just now as frequently as Bossuet or Pascal, adopt the role of great reconciler of Frenchmen. There was a certain naïvety in all this, and a touch of sentimentality on the part of a man who had taken sixty years to discover the existence of his country's work-force. But he was not blind to the dangers that threatened the realisation of his vision of a united nation. There were still Vichy diehards who refused to accept the new order.[105] There was still a considerable section of the community committed to Maurrassian or Fascist doctrines.[106] Most cruelly to himself, he had to admit the entrenched right-wing attitudes of so many leaders of the Church. 'Si on leur ouvrait le cœur,' he remarked, 'on y trouverait gravé le nom de Vichy.'[107] The old question of France's educational system—the rival claims of state and religious schools—could crop up again as an obstacle to concord: and he himself insisted, somewhat defensively, that Catholics, though they must reject the divisive parallelism of France's 'deux jeunesses', could not accept the kind of radical reform of the écoles libres that some socialist theorists demanded.[108]

Just as great as the confidence with which Mauriac addressed himself to these matters was the authority which was his at this juncture of his life. To the Left, he was respected as the only great bourgeois writer, the only member of the Academy, to espouse their cause, join the C.N.E., give support to *Les Lettres françaises*. To de Gaulle, always alert to the need to bestow a cultural legitimacy on his regime by the support of influential men of letters, Mauriac, as an exception to the Academy's refusal to honour the Resistance, was a figure of some utility. He showed his favour by inviting Mauriac to accompany him on his triumphant tour of the newly liberated Eastern regions.[109] But prestige brought its problems. This attractiveness of Mauriac to each of the adversaries in the post-war power struggle was a source of considerable tension. The moment of showdown had arrived between de Gaulle and the Communists, those hard-headed plotters whom the General had always distinguished from the 'poètes de l'action' who had worked with them in the Resistance.[110] Mauriac, paying regular ecstatic tribute to 'le premier des nôtres', yet still a member of both the C.N.E. and the Front National, had a foot in each camp.

An important source of information on this situation is Claude Mauriac's diary, published under the title *Un autre de Gaulle*. The novelist's elder son was de Gaulle's personal secretary from the Liberation until October 1948, and to him de Gaulle expressed his displeasure at the presence of François Mauriac on the administrative committee of the Front National and at his continuing support, often as a major speaker, of their rallies. Mauriac must know, de Gaulle complained to Claude, that he was aiding an organisation that was working against France.[111] In his book on de Gaulle, written some twenty years later, Mauriac explains: 'Je me trouvais empêtré dans le filet que tenait fortement le parti communiste', and he implies strongly that he was desperately anxious to leave the Front at the earliest possible moment.[112] Why, then, did he not do so? Why did he stand for re-election to the movement's committee early in 1945?[113] The Dominican Father Bruckberger, former almoner of the F.F.I., unwittingly provides a plausible answer in his account of the period. He relates a confrontation between Mauriac and Albert Camus in October 1944, just after the latter, along with Bruckberger himself, had resigned from the C.N.E. in protest at its transformation into a Communist band-wagon. Challenged by Camus to explain his continued adhesion to the group, Mauriac replied, in keeping with the spirit of his articles of the time, 'C'est par solidarité'. 'Non, M. Mauriac,' Bruckberger reports Camus as retorting. 'C'est par peur.

Vous avez peur d'eux et c'est pourquoi vous vous laisserez mener où ils voudront.' And Mauriac is said to have admitted: 'C'est pourtant vrai.'[114]

Mauriac was certainly, at this time, behind the apparent optimism of his writings, a frightened man. But to say this is not to endorse the criticism which Bruckberger's hostile account levels at him. On the contrary, his courage in the face of numerous threats on his life—threats kept secret until the appearance of his son's memoirs—deserves recognition. Claude describes his father as a man prepared for death, dependent more than ever on the support of his religious faith.[115] The threats came from both the Right—occasioned by such events as the assassination by members of the Resistance Council of the former Vichy Information Minister Philippe Henriot[116]—and the Left, when Mauriac protested against the excesses of the post-war purge.[117] In such a delicate situation, when abandonment of the Front National would, as Claude Mauriac says, turn the whole of the left-wing press against him[118] and be seen as a betrayal, proof that the old leopard still had his bourgeois spots, it is plain that to stand still as Mauriac did, was as safe a policy as any. As early as October 1944, Claude had helped him draft a letter of resignation from the Front;[119] but many months would elapse before the climate cooled sufficiently for him to fade discreetly out of the group's activities. This failure of one of his cherished hopes—a lasting reconciliation of Catholic and Communist —must have disillusioned him deeply.

His dream of a great national unity was, in fact, very short-lived. Even before the last German left Paris, Frenchman was killing Frenchman in unofficial civil war. Most of the dead—the total number of which has been estimated at around 40,000[120]—were the victims of private executions. Others died as a result of sentences passed by the Haute Cour which de Gaulle had instituted for the purpose of restraining the anarchy of uncontrolled vendettas. This formal purge, known as the épuration, again brought Mauriac into conflict both with the Left and with de Gaulle.

In retrospect, and with typical enthusiasm for the neat antithesis, Mauriac said that he defended the collaborators after the war as fervently as he had attacked them during it.[121] Inevitably, this is too simple a picture. His articles of the time show that, while he was opposed to a widespread, indiscriminate and prolonged purge, he firmly believed in punishing the guilty. 'Il ne s'agit pas ici de plaider pour les coupables', he declared in September 1944. But he warned that many people whose guilt was not proven were in danger of suffering the same fate as the guilty.[122] These same sentiments were expressed a month later in an article, which, long before Anouilh's play *Pauvre Bitos*, pursued the analogy between the *épuration* and the purges of Robespierre.[123] In December he argued that, while those proven guilty of having betrayed their compatriots to the Gestapo merited punishment by death, not all the supporters of the Vichy regime were guilty in this way.[124] And in January 1945 he stated that the *épuration* was probably an inevitable evil, but an evil nevertheless, and one that had to be ended as soon as possible.[125] He argued in addition that the legal basis of the purge needed clarification, for the law by which one man was condemned to death and another to imprisonment seemed as random in its operation as a lottery.[126] The issue was further complicated by the apparent international recognition of Vichy, manifested by the presence in Pétain's capital of the American and Russian ambassadors, as well as that of the papal nuncio.[127] Mauriac believed that it was impossible to blame the majority of Vichy supporters in the light of these circumstances, and he campaigned for amnesty for all those not actually guilty of bloodshed or denunciation to the Germans.[128] He pointed out also that the very judges who passed sentence on the collaborators had themselves sworn allegiance to Pétain as head of the established state.[129]

Mauriac's involvement in the *épuration* debate was seen in conflicting lights, according to the standpoint of the commentator. To many he was Saint François des Assises, intervening in the name of Christian charity and on grounds sentimental more than rational.[130] Many left-wingers were cynical and angry about what they regarded as unduly delicate sentiments, and only an intervention by Jacques Debû-Bridel, who argued that such a reaction was to be expected from a Christian and should not obscure Mauriac's record during the Occupation, prevented the resultant clash from costing Mauriac his place on the committee of the Front National.[131] To others, however, Mauriac's feelings did not seem so noble. He has been described in a more sinister light as a man, at best, trying to cultivate an image of goodness for posterity;[132] at worst, because he was thought to defend some of the accused with less than maximum vigour, seeking revenge for set-backs to his electoral schemes within the Academy.[133] On the whole, these attacks reveal more about the prejudices of their formulators than about the truth of the events. But some discussion is needed of the issues raised by Pol Vandromme when he writes of Mauriac:

Mais il choisit ses réprouvés comme des femmes d'oeuvres
qui ont *leurs* pauvres. Il protégea quelques-uns de ses confrères,
mais il fit le silence (et son silence en disait long) sur les autres.
Par exemple, il ne souffla mot lorsqu'on condamna le maréchal
Pétain et Charles Maurras.[134]

As far as Maurras is concerned, there is no doubt that Mauriac
believed that severe punishment was necessary for this man with
whom his own relationship had for so long hung in the balance, this
former champion of the nation who had settled in the end for humili-
ating truce. Commenting on the death sentence passed on Abel
Hermant, whom he had unsuccessfully tried to defend, he reflected
how much more deplorable than Hermant's had been the influence of
Maurras.[135] But, from a horror of bloodshed (says Claude Mauriac[136]),
he supported the plea for clemency initiated by his son after Maurras'
original death-sentence, and was relieved to see this commuted to one
of life imprisonment. In Pétain's case, Vandromme's allegations of
Mauriac's silence are simply untrue. In July 1945 Mauriac reminded
his readers (perhaps none too convincingly) that, in coming to terms
with Nazi Germany, Pétain had merely done what Daladier and
Chamberlain had tried to do in 1938.[137] The following month he
again insisted on the Marshal's noble intentions and recommended
mercy to the jury and judges.[138] And after the death sentence was
passed he expressed the hope, as in the case of Maurras, that it would
never be implemented.[139] Thus there is no basis for accusing Mauriac
of lacking in mercy towards the man for whom he had expressed
admiration, albeit limited, in 1940.

A notable success of Mauriac's was his defence of Henri Béraud.[140]
Also, he was a signatory of a petition organised by Louis Guitard,
successfully, on behalf of Maurice Bardèche.[141] This did not prevent
Bardèche, in a bitter open letter, from accusing Mauriac of being a
narrow-minded man, blinded by naïve admiration for the Resistance
and by his scorn for all non-resistants—attitudes which fanned the
flames of the very *épuration* that he was hypocritically pretending to
restrain.[142] Bardèche's case is excessive; but the background to his
attack on Mauriac is a reminder of the most controversial issue arising
from the latter's involvement in the purge: namely, the sentence and
execution of Bardèche's brother-in-law, the novelist and critic Robert
Brasillach.

In the list of thirteen hundred reprieves granted by de Gaulle as
provisional Head of government, there figured the names of many

writers. An exception was that of Brasillach. 'Je ne me sentis pas le droit de gracier,' de Gaulle explains in his memoirs. 'Car, dans les lettres comme en tout, le talent est un titre de responsabilité.'[143] Even Claude Mauriac, passionately committed against the capital punishment of collaborators, agreed that Brasillach's record of collaboration spoke for itself.[144] It included the denunciation of François Mauriac to the Germans in the pages of *Je suis partout*. But Mauriac, again according to his son, was pierced to the heart by Brasillach's trial and sentence. And when Claude drew up a petition in favour of a reprieve, his father took it upon himself to circulate this within the Academy, bringing a moving letter of gratitude from the condemned man. Mauriac then went further: he went to see de Gaulle in person to plead for his fellow writer's life. What took place on this occasion is unclear. Louis Guitard alleges that de Gaulle promised to spare Brasillach, then changed his mind, incurring on Mauriac's part a deep resentment against which he had to struggle later.[145] Robert Aron, in his more objective account, says that Mauriac gleaned from de Gaulle the strong impression that a reprieve would be accorded, and that, on the same night, Mauriac said as much during a dinner at the Russian Embassy, only to be hastily silenced by the embarrassed Foreign Minister, Bidault.[146] Claude Mauriac's diary, however, shows that Mauriac and Bidault were the guests of Ambassador Bogomolov two days *before* his father's visit to de Gaulle.[147] It goes on to confirm, nevertheless, that de Gaulle implied to Mauriac that Brasillach would not die. The version which Mauriac himself gives is simply that de Gaulle made no firm promise.[148]

Whether this unhappy story brought about a cooling of Mauriac's ardour towards de Gaulle will probably never be known. What is clear is that the General's whole attitude to the purge was a source of disappointment to him. 'Si le pouvoir de cet homme nous est connu pour assurer au dehors la grandeur de la patrie,' he wrote,

> les passions qui le déchirent au dedans, on dirait parfois qu'il
> ne veut pas les entendre. Debout à son poste de vigie, entre la
> mer et les étoiles, il ne tourne pas la tête vers nous. On pourrait
> le croire inattentif aux querelles de l'équipage, aux haines
> séculaires que nos derniers malheurs ont sinistrement rajeunies.
> Les ignore-t-il? L'a-t-il reconnu ce bruit des fusils déchargés
> (. . .)? Nous ne savons pas non plus s'il demeure insensible à ces
> remous de l'opinion autour des verdicts qui se succèdent,
> indulgents ou impitoyables.[149]

Claude Mauriac, in the privacy of his diary, allowed himself a more positive expression of misgivings than his father's public rhetorical questioning. The policy of the present government, he said, in which he had had such high hopes, was firmly based on hypocrisy, deception and vengeance.[150] François Mauriac, however, was loath to criticise de Gaulle too outspokenly. The purge horrified him; but how much more horrible would be an escalation of the differences of opinion towards it into a new and perhaps irrevocable split between former Resistance allies. 'Je ne voudrais pas ici écrire un seul mot,' he hastened to say in his article on de Gaulle's apparent aloofness from everyday justice, 'qui pût irriter les passions, puisque mon ardent désir est d'aider, pour mon humble part, à la réconciliation nationale'.[151] Conscious of the authority that was his, he sought to use it with the utmost responsibility.

(iv) *Mauriac and de Gaulle: first contacts*

The first exhilaration of the Liberation had inspired Mauriac to eulogies of de Gaulle that would have embarrassed almost any other public figure than this one. De Gaulle had given his person to France, been a lone symbol of hope, inspiring Frenchmen by his radio broadcasts in his 'prophetic' voice. This young chief had been the first, Mauriac claimed (helping to establish one of the more durable Gaullist myths), to understand the conditions of modern mobilised warfare. He was possessed of a 'réalité intemporelle'. Mauriac 'devoured with his eyes' this walking illustration from Guizot's *History of France*, this providential leader, proof of God's special protection for blessed France, this man who by some mysterious predestination had inherited the very name of ancient Gaul. France had several times in the past, he argued, turned in hours of need or fear to a strong man. But de Gaulle was not the classic 'man on horseback', no seductive Boulanger to win over the nation for the furtherance of his own ambitions. He was no *prince-président*, no Bonapartist dictator, but on the contrary a man committed to liberty, resolved to hand back power to the people—to *all* of the people, not just a privileged few. He had defended the Republic against the vilifications of the Maurrassians and thus rallied men like Mauriac himself to the cause of a regime for which they never had much love. The symbol of the Resistance and the core of French unity, he would now restore that justice at home that was the first step to the re-creation of national prestige abroad.[152]

This public projection was a compound of relief, gratitude,

romanticism, wishful thinking and the more realistic comprehension that to play a part in the creation of a glorious image of the General around which men could rally might positively serve the cause of unity. Even when this early post-Liberation period was over, and when the rigours of the *épuration* had suppressed some of his initial hopes, Mauriac was unwilling to erode in any way the legend to which he had contributed. De Gaulle, even an inhuman de Gaulle, indifferent to the inequalities of the purge, was the best guarantor of unity.

It was commonly held that Mauriac was much closer to de Gaulle than he really was. Claude Mauriac writes that his father was rumoured to be a kind of behind-the-scenes Information Minister, expressing de Gaulle's views before they were made public so as to test public reaction to them. Yet, he testifies, Mauriac had only met the General twice—at two meals, and never unaccompanied.[153] These meetings, and the later meeting when Mauriac went to plead for Brasillach, had been enough to create certain doubts in his mind. On the face of it, there promised to be a good deal of common ground between the two men. Of similar age (Mauriac was five years older), they came from much the same class background, in which a fervently patriotic outlook was a part of the birthright. Both, to some degree, could now be seen to have diverged from the views of their social class, in so far as Vichy, which both had combated, had had that class's majority support. Each had declared the opinion that the working class must be rewarded for its part in the Resistance; but the separate reasons that underlay this common view point to a considerable gulf between the two men. Mauriac's warmth towards the proletariat in 1944–1945 contained a large dose of sentimentality; de Gaulle, on the other hand, was totally pragmatic. He realised, as he says in his memoirs, that explosive wage demands were bound to follow the Liberation, for wage levels had been severely depressed during the war; not to yield to these pressures, not to institute 'socialist' legislation —nationalisation of key industries and banks, larger family allowances —was to hand the working class vote to the Communists.[154] Indeed, that de Gaulle had little true feeling for the aspirations of workers is shown by his comment in *Le Salut* that Vichy's corporatist industrial system had been a step in the right direction.[155] He was nearer to Pétain than to Léon Blum on such issues, as his speech at St.-Étienne in 1948, in the R.P.F. days, was to confirm. So that Mauriac's somewhat naïve question at their first meeting, as to what de Gaulle proposed to

do about the financial domination of the Trusts, should be greeted by
a dismissive snort,[156] is not without significance. And despite having
described de Gaulle as a defender of the Republic against the ideology
of Maurras, Mauriac had to admit to his son that the General was after
all very much in the Maurrassian mould. Mauriac, not without reason,
felt intimidated by de Gaulle during these first encounters. Not only
was he dazzled by the man in the way he ecstatically describes in his
De Gaulle, but also he felt faced with a creature of a quite different
species, 'un cormoran (. . .) qui parlait cormoran'. De Gaulle, he told
Claude after the discussion about Brasillach, was a master, but 'un
maître sans complaisance ni faiblesse, et tout de même d'une race qui
n'est pas à notre mesure'. But such clashes of personality—marking
the gulf between the weathered statesman and the fledgling journalist
—did not prevent Mauriac from continuing to express publicly his
total allegiance to the man. Claude, whose impressions of de Gaulle
at this time were very similar to his father's, summed up the position
of both Mauriacs when he wrote in his diary that the General had to
be supported, no matter how disappointing his performance, if hopes
of peace and unity were to survive.[157] Claude housed private doubts
about de Gaulle's potential dictatorial designs.[158] His father, on the
other hand, dismissed such fears, reiterating his view, in reaction to a
speech by Léon Blum, that de Gaulle was no Bonaparte, much less a
Mussolini or a Hitler.[159] He was sincere in his wish, said Mauriac on
the fifth anniversary of the June 18th message, to serve the nation, not
to exploit its favours.[160]

Serving the nation, in 1945, meant helping to find a viable constitutional basis for recovery. The uneasy situation in the immediate
post-war period, with de Gaulle as the provisional arbiter of an
assembly dominated by the groups that had emerged triumphant from
the Resistance—the Communists, the Socialists and the new Catholic
party, the Mouvement républicain populaire—was in urgent need of
resolution. What, precisely, were to be the constitutional relationships
between these disparate elements: a president scornful of parliamentary
democracy and of the *régime des partis*, a totalitarian party whose
allegiance to any eventual constitution must be highly problematic, a
party that had shared in the humiliation of the Third Republic, and a
new group of largely untried politicians? This was a question on
which Mauriac, at first and on grounds of inexperience and even lack
of interest in such 'technical' matters, was loath to commit himself:

Retour à la constitution de 1875? Assemblée constituante

souveraine? Ce débat pourrait être académique. (. . .) Pour moi,
je demeure incertain et en éprouve quelque honte; car un
journaliste, c'est son métier que d'avoir réponse à tout et que de
savoir ce qu'il faut penser sur chaque chose. Le problème
constitutionnel ne m'a jamais beaucoup occupé, voilà mon
excuse. J'ai toujours eu l'idée que ce ne sont pas les institutions
qui corrompent les hommes, que ce sont, au contraire, les
hommes qui corrompent les institutions.

No system would be perfect: 'A quelque parti qu'on s'arrête, il faudra
vivre dans l'odeur d'une chambre de malade.' Thus, probably, the
outcome of the debate was of secondary importance to the good-will
of the participants when it came to making the eventual constitution
work.[161] But more thought on the matter led Mauriac to lean, some
three months afterwards, in favour of a reinforced presidency. The
president would, naturally, be de Gaulle, and he would be

défendu par la Constitution contre les bourrasques et les sautes
d'humeur de l'Assemblée, et aussi défendu contre lui-même,
parce qu'il connaîtrait les limites exactes de ses prérogatives et de
ses droits.

De Gaulle's aloofness, or rather his 'purity', his lack of partisanship
suited him perfectly to the role of head of state, Mauriac argued.[162]
But how this envisaged balance of powers—a strong but not absol-
utely sovereign assembly, and an equally strong but 'controlled'
presidency—would function in detail, he did not explain. In any case,
his proposal was clearly too much of a compromise to suit either de
Gaulle or the parliamentarians.

The rumour of the imminent retirement from politics of the
frustrated General, increasingly strong as the winter of 1945 drew on,
was heard with great regret by Mauriac. De Gaulle's departure, he
wrote, would deprive France of her last chance of regaining a leading
role in world affairs.[163] When the expected resignation came, in
January 1946, he greeted the news with cries of lament, especially in
his article 'Les Trois contradictions', published in Le Figaro on
February 14th. De Gaulle, he said, had been caught in three traps.
Firstly, the economic one, into which he had fallen by his decision—
wholly justifiable in itself—to concentrate on France's military
renewal, to buy for France a place among Germany's conquerors in
the last months of the war, which had meant neglecting vital domestic
reconstruction. Secondly, de Gaulle's hunger for independence for his
country had led him to take less than full account of her inevitable

dependence on her Allies. Thirdly, there was the old bugbear of the parties, which Mauriac, in this moment of bitterness, blamed above all, as did de Gaulle himself, for the great man's departure. 'Et maintenant', wrote Mauriac, almost scornfully,

> tout est rentré au sérail dans l'ordre accoutumé. Même sur les caricatures, on ne voit plus cet homme qui avait l'audace de dépasser tous les autres et de marcher la tête dans les étoiles. Que les partis reposent en paix dans le sentiment délicieux de l'égalité retrouvée! Voici revenu le temps des chefs interchangeables. (...) Nous trouverons autant d'hommes qu'il nous en faudra pour cette période (brève, espérons-le!) de l'Histoire où il sera nécessaire que la France consente à s'effacer un peu et à se mettre en veilleuse.[164]

The immediate result of this sympathetic article was an invitation to Mauriac to visit de Gaulle at Marly, where he was living before his retreat to Colombey. According to Claude Mauriac's record of what his father told him of this meeting, de Gaulle not only gave his views on Mauriac's recent article—he had over-stated France's economic plight, the General told him, and under-rated the degree of independence that France had regained—but laid before him for the first time his conception of the government he believed the nation to need. It is an eloquent testimony to the importance that Mauriac had achieved as a commentator and in the sight of the General that he should be made privy at this early stage, four months before the famous Bayeux speech, to the ideas that were to be embodied in the constitution of the Fifth Republic. The President really *would* have powers, exclaimed Mauriac to Claude afterwards.[165]

It seems certain, however, that despite the disparaging view of the parties—a throw-back to Mauriac's pre-war attitudes—that the General's departure had led him to express, he was more alarmed than thrilled by what de Gaulle had told him, and that the Marly meeting was important in his determination to give parliamentary democracy his support in the ensuing years. The memory of Fascist dictatorships and the tragic embroilment of Catholics in the onslaught on democracy were all too recent for Mauriac to find de Gaulle's vision of personal rule palatable. Within a few months, he was saying to his son, after the unexpected M.R.P. successes in the June elections: 'Entre un homme—aussi grand soit-il—et un tel rassemblement, je n'hésiterais pas une minute à choisir—s'il faut choisir.'[166] Claude's growing anxiety, as 1946 wore on, at de Gaulle's increasingly frequent refer-

ences to himself as a monarch in exile—references naturally passed on
to his father—was certainly shared by the elder Mauriac. At the end of
September there occurred what Claude, still loyal in spite of his
qualms to the man he continued to serve as personal secretary, called
Mauriac's 'abandonment' (*abandon*) of de Gaulle. This took the form of
an article called 'La Recherche de l'absolu' (not republished in any of
the collections) in which Mauriac gave his support to the new draft
constitution which made provision for strictly limited presidential
powers.[167] And when the result of the referendum on the constitutional proposals was known, he angrily, in private, criticised de
Gaulle, whose campaign had made many M.R.P. supporters vote 'No'
against the directives and interests of their party.[168]

On New Year's Day 1947 Mauriac made his disappointment with
de Gaulle public when he reflected ironically on his own earlier faith
in him:

> Que n'échafaudons-nous pas dans ces songeries où nous
> accommodons les événements et les êtres selon nos goûts
> particuliers! C'est une manie à laquelle on cède encore à mon
> âge. Nous nous plaisions, par exemple, à imaginer ce que devait
> être l'action politique du généneral de Gaulle, et nous avons la
> naïveté d'être surpris qu'il ait réagi aux circonstances de la
> manière que nous n'attendions pas. Quand j'étais enfant,
> j'inscrivais au bas de mon addition n'importe quel chiffre et
> j'étais assez fou pour croire que ce serait peut-être le bon; mais
> il est aussi fou de se représenter dans les moindres détails le
> comportement d'un homme, comme s'il n'était pas le résultat de
> réflexions, de sentiments, de calculs imprévisibles et dont presque
> tout nous échappe. Nous passons notre temps à être déçus par
> l'écart entre ce que nous espérons et ce qui arrive, comme si cet
> écart pouvait ne pas être immense.'[169]

Two months later, Mauriac's suspicions were further aroused[170]
by de Gaulle's speech at Bruneval, especially its notoriously cryptic
final sentence—a prophecy of a revolt of the people against the 'sterile
games' and 'ill-constructed framework' of the Fourth Republic, a
prophecy which smacked to many of a call to a *coup d'état*.[171] The
ensuing creation by de Gaulle of the Rassemblement du Peuple français was the final blow to what remained of Mauriac's allegiance to
the General. Contrary to its aim of unifying the nation by an all-party
alliance of those who believed in a Gaullist future for France, regardless of class or economic outlook, Mauriac saw the R.P.F. from the

outset as likely to have a divisive influence, repugnant to the Communist working class[172] and out of touch with the Resistance Left in general.[173] It would finally shatter all hopes of unity by becoming primarily a right-wing movement[174] and de Gaulle himself, he believed, would be inevitably drawn into the very struggle of parties which he abominated.[175] By 1949 Mauriac's reflections on de Gaulle were definitely tinged with an acid sense of the might-have-been: had de Gaulle stayed on, and had he fought against certain tendencies in his nature. . . .[176] And two years later, he commented that de Gaulle, in any event, probably lacked the strength to surmount the obstacles he would have encountered. The Gaullist dream, he made it clear, was over:

> Nous avions un homme tout à coup, qui avait fait réellement quelque chose, qui incarnait la liberté et l'honneur pour une moitié de la France et une promesse d'ordre pour l'autre. Je ne doutais pas que cet homme n'entreprît de faire précisément ce que j'aurais fait à sa place. Je ne tenais aucun compte des espaces interstellaires qui séparent le cerveau d'un général français de celui d'un bourgeois libéral, poète et inventeur de fictions (. . .)
>
> Que le reste lui ait échappé, qu'il n'ait pas su ou pas pu ou pas voulu accomplir ce qui me paraissait d'une exécution si simple dans mes songeries de ce moment-là, compte pour peu si sa volonté eût été inefficace contre l'inextricable réseau de conjonctures imprévisibles où viennent s'anéantir immanquablement les rêves des hommes.'[177]

(v) Communists and Catholics

One of the three pillars on which Mauriac had built his post-war hopes had fallen. What of the other two: his sense of fraternity with the Communists of the Resistance and his excitement at the emergence of a new Catholic movement? Towards the Communists, his viewpoint changed dramatically—and, in retrospect, inevitably, in the months and years that followed the Liberation. Maurice Schumann described Mauriac's attitude to the Communists as 'une répulsion nuancée par la tendresse',[178] a phrase which captures the conflicting elements in that attitude, but which might suggest that they remained in static opposition to each other. The fact is that whatever sympathy Mauriac felt for the Communists in 1944 and 1945—based on what he saw as their struggle for human dignity and for France against the invaders[179]—was gradually replaced by a hatred of Communists abroad and a scorn of those in France. In January 1945, he was still ready to belittle the Russian threat to Western Europe. 'Nous saluons', he wrote, 'sans l'ombre d'une arrière-pensée, la victoire des armées rouges qui délivre l'Europe.'[180] But by July of the same year, he saw the tensions of the encroaching Cold War as a terrible danger— 'l'épouvantail', he called it.[181] Yet he still felt that the Communists' part in the Resistance entitled them to a share in government.[182] But as his eyes opened to the realities of Stalinist Russia, his horror of the Soviet regime increased,[183] until his attitude towards French Communists as well as their Russian and East European counterparts was one of bitter opposition. In January 1946, when de Gaulle's departure seemed to create a vacuum into which the Communists might step, he expressed his fear of the absorption of the Socialists into the Communist party and of the destruction of the Left's commitment to human rights that this would involve.[184] A few months later he mocked the futility of the P.C.F.'s position of having to share in a coalition government and thus suspend its revolutionary and totalitarian principles.[185] He derided French Communists as puppets of Moscow.[186] He saw their position as untenable, by virtue of their French nationality and hence their belonging to 'une race spirituelle que haïssent vos maîtres slaves et asiatiques'.[187] The French Communist intellectual was in a particular dilemma, by membership of a party which denied him the right to think for himself.[188]

In spite of these repeated attacks, he was fascinated by the nature of Communism's opposition to the Christian faith, stemming, as he saw it, from 'l'idée que nous nous faisons de la personne humaine'.[189] This basic difference could only be resolved by recognising the supremacy of the Gospels over *Das Kapital*.[190] Yet, on occasions, remembering the wartime alliances of Christian and Communist, he felt that the latter's capacity for self-sacrifice in the name of a higher cause was a possible starting-point for reconciliation. It was this love of a great cause

> qui, dans l'âme des meilleurs communistes, purifie le marxisme de sa primitive erreur, de ses dégénérescences et de ses perversions. (. . .) Et c'est le miracle d'une réconciliation et de ce qui semblait le plus irréductible: le matérialisme et Dieu. Les contradictions se concilient sans peine au coeur des simples assoiffés de vérité et de justice.[191]

The task of transposing such a reconciliation to the political plane was one for which Mauriac saw no practical method; and indeed he made it clear in *La Pierre d'achoppement* that he saw the fraternity of men on opposite sides of this particular fence as possible only on a personal, non-party level.[192] Even this limited optimism was to disappear. In 1956, he wrote that de-Stalinisation had changed nothing: religious faith was still a prime target of Communists, and when they said it was not there was always some good tactical reason in their minds.[193]

Thus Mauriac's hopes of unity in this area were discarded like so many other hopes. It must be said that his own prolonged and often petty journalistic squabbles with the Communist writers Pierre Hervé and Pierre Courtade[194] destroyed any chance that he himself may have had, on either the personal or political plane, of exemplifying charity and understanding towards his Marxist adversaries. He was un-questionably ruffled by the success of Hervé in particular in laying bare the reversal of his attitudes to the Communists since 1944. The truth was, as both Mauriac and Hervé knew, that the former had simply rediscovered his own voice. The revolutionary rhetoric of the heady post-Liberation days had never sounded convincing in such a patrician mouth. Very soon Mauriac had gravitated towards the role of liberal reformer rather than play the part of a revolutionary over-thrower of institutions. He had revealed this both in the perennial debate over the maintenance of the *écoles libres*[195] and also in the dis-cussion of the future of the French Academy—for which Mauriac, despite the unsavoury record of many of its laureates, saw no need of radical change.[196]

His true place, it was clear, was with a liberal centre-left party, non-doctrinaire in economic and social outlook, but committed to the moral, humanitarian and Christian values that he had consistently up-held in public since 1935. This party he found—or for a number of years thought he had found—in the M.R.P., which came to replace both de Gaulle and the Left as the focal point of his attention. Though never a member of the party, he claimed to have voted for it in every election between the end of the war and January 1956.[197] He saw in its leaders, Teitgen, Parodi and especially Bidault, the spiritual descen-dants of Lamennais, Lacordaire and Montalembert; and in the party itself he hailed the fruition of the Christian democratic tradition reflected in the Sillon and now made possible by the collapse of re-actionary Catholic power-groups like the Action Française.[198] He praised the M.R.P. for its desire to dissociate Catholics from 'le christianisme politique' and from an expressly pro-clerical position, for its denunciation of Catholic movements that had merely utilised

Christian support for political ends.[199] Above all, the M.R.P. was conscious of a mission to satisfy a demand for honesty and purity in public life, and to 'rendre leur Seigneur aux foules qui L'ont perdu, qui ne savent où on L'a mis, et qui Le cherchent'.[200] It was during this period of enthusiasm for the M.R.P. that he reminded his readers so often of his association with the Sillon and labelled himself as a life-long Christian democrat. He even had the satisfaction of conferring on Marc Sangnier himself the insignia of the Legion of Honour.[201]

But yet again his hopes were to be dashed. His enthusiasm for the M.R.P. was already on the wane by April 1946, when he described the party as 'le cher M.R.P., vêtu d'une probité de moins en moins candide et d'un lin qui n'a peut-être plus toute la blancheur de ses commencements'.[202] His New Year hope for 1947 was that the party would not forget its Christian responsibilities, but the danger signs, he implied, were already evident.[203] That he saw a spiritual role, founded on Christian example, as being of greater importance to the M.R.P. than electoral success is shown by his reaction to the setbacks suffered by the party during 1947. He expressed the feeling that the Christian democrats were too innocent for the dirty infighting of politics and that their real destiny was not to govern but to guard French Catholicism from the influence of the reactionary Right—which they could do just as well in opposition as in power.[204] But the next few years were to see Mauriac losing faith in their ability to realise even this more limited aim. His growing criticism of the M.R.P. leaders became an important element in that wider opposition, more vociferous as the years passed, to the Fourth Republic and all its works.

(vi) *Scourge of the Fourth Republic*

Mauriac's overriding concern on the purely political plane, it had by now emerged, was with the prestige of France, with her ability, especially in the eyes of foreigners, to live up to the Christian and humanitarian traditions which he saw as the bedrock of her national identity. Her dealings with other countries and with her colonial dependencies were crucial in this respect, and thus Mauriac focussed his attention, during the Fourth Republic, on foreign and colonial affairs. From the last months of the war he had looked hopefully forward to a future in which France could reassert herself in the world, stay independent of the two giant power-blocs,[205] give a lead to the nations of the Third World and also to Europe—a role she could claim as hers because of her sense of a spiritual mission.[206] To these

ends, she must avoid identifying herself too closely with the cause of
either West or East. 'Il y a deux matous,' he warned when people saw
danger only in the Soviet bloc.[207] Alliance with the West, given
France's post-war economic dependence, was inevitable,[208] but he
welcomed also, as a balancing factor, the Franco-Soviet alliance of
1944.[209] Neither tie, he insisted, should entail servitude.[210]

   As his attitude to the Communists hardened, he became gradually
more sympathetic to the idea of a Western Alliance. Deciding in 1947
that his hope that the French Communist party might provide the
liaison between the adversaries in the Cold War was just a pipe-
dream,[211] he had evolved by 1950 to a definite anti-neutralist and pro-
American stand:

> Parlons net: mettre dans le même sac, comme le font nos
> 'neutralistes', les États-Unis d'Amérique et la Russie des Soviets
> revient à considérer qu'une libre démocratie ne vaut pas mieux
> qu'un État totalitaire.[212]

His withdrawal from this position over the next few years was something he attributed to changing circumstances in the balance of world
power, notably the diminished threat of Russian aggression in Western
Europe.[213] Yet it is difficult not to attribute it, as least in part, to a
growing anti-American—and, in the favoured French term, anti-
Anglo-Saxon—tendency, temporarily suspended, through fear of
Russia, around 1950. Already, at the end of the war, his formal pro-
clamations of admiration for Britain and of a belief in the primacy of
Anglo-French co-operation were interspersed with complaints of
Britain's supposed lack of charity towards France[214] and, more important, of the Allies' unwillingness to grant the demands of de Gaulle:
for a rebuff for de Gaulle, he declared, was a rebuff for France.[215]
These blows to Mauriac's sense of France's importance were the
starting-point for his later aversion to the Anglo-Saxons. In 1945
his attitude was already ambiguous. Expressing his admiration for
Britain's achievements in the war, he warned that the benevolent face
of Britain was rapidly vanishing in favour of the old familiar counten-
ance of the ancient enemy—was not the Franco-British clash in Syria
a sign of this? However, as well as decrying the Anglophiles who
urged France to closer ties with Britain—'à leur insu', he remarked,
'ils obéissent aux mêmes réflexes que les collaborateurs de naguère'—
he attacked also the excessive Anglophobes, the 'maniacs' who were
incapable of forgetting Joan of Arc, St. Helena, Fachoda and Mers-el-
Kebir.[216] Even if he had not so perfectly reversed this position later, in

recalling perfidious Albion's infamous record—'le bûcher de Rouen', St. Helena, the dum-dum bullet used against the Boers[217]—his own Anglophobia, based largely on such selective historical echoes, would not be hard to prove. Britain and the U.S.A.—for like de Gaulle and like a large section of French opinion generally, Mauriac scarcely distinguished between the two nations—had been insensitive to French feelings in their bombing of German installations in Normandy,[218] they constituted the greatest obstacle to world peace,[219] and their pragmatic policies ignored all moral laws,[220] incapable as they were of the 'regard désintéressé' that traditionally shone on the world from the face of France.[221] More particularly, in spite of warnings from the French, Britain was largely to blame for both world wars, while America too had contributed to creating the conditions in which the Second World War had come about.[222] The Americans, furthermore, had erred, he said, in recognising the Vichy regime[223] —although he overlooked here the fact that this recognition had furnished him with an argument in defence of certain alleged collaborators.

Ultimately, in spite of statements to the contrary, Mauriac nursed a deep resentment of France's Western allies that drove him to look to the continent of Europe in the hope of finding friends there. He expressed his interest in the idea of a federal Europe, based on cultural as well as economic ties, independent of both East and West, and in which France would play a leading role.[224] His one great misgiving concerning Europe centred on the old enemy, Germany, to whose possible rearmament he declared his opposition on a number of occasions.[225]

In contrast to his general willingness to see a newly organised Europe, Mauriac's initial attitude to France's overseas territories in the post-war years was a conservative one. Although he could decry the imperialism of other nations, he was in favour of maintaining the status quo in the French Empire, and for him the resurgent Arab nationalism in France's North African colonies was simply '(le) fanatisme islamique'.[226] None of his views was to change more radically than this one, however, in the course of the next few years. For although the gradual diminution of the Empire caused him lasting regret, he was soon to be known as a friend of the Moslems. '(Il) a quelque chance', jeered Pol Vandromme, 'de finir sa vie dans la peau d'un musulman.'[227] It was during the Moroccan crisis of 1952 that Mauriac adopted the controversial position that re-established him, after five or six years of relatively minor impact on the public scene, as an important political commentator. He attributed his public stance over Morocco to the recent award of the Nobel Prize, which made him feel obliged to commit himself more fully in such matters.[228] Under his presidency, the Centre Catholique des Intellectuels Français demanded an enquiry into the events in Casablanca, which was refused. The incident sparked off press warfare, with many Catholics in Rabat attacking Mauriac.[229]

Mauriac's critical view of government policy in Morocco was so remote from that of Le Figaro that there now occurred the first in a series of transfers of his regular journalistic contributions. In spite of his continuing friendship with Le Figaro's editor Pierre Brisson, Mauriac began to write more frequently for La Table ronde. He had published his 'Bloc-notes' in this paper since October 1952, but following his partial severance with Le Figaro, they became more overtly political. Very soon, however, he clashed with the right-wing and bien-pensant directors of La Table ronde, and from November 1953 the 'Bloc-notes' appeared in a new review, the radical L'Express, with whose contributors he had, once again, little in common save for a growing scorn for the men of the Fourth Republic.

Meanwhile he accepted the presidency of France-Maghreb, an association for the reconciliation of French Catholics and Moroccan Moslems. It was here that, together with men like Louis Massignon, the liberal General Catroux, the Sorbonne teachers Julien and Blachère and Robert Barrat, author of Justice pour le Maroc, Mauriac campaigned for his new cause. He denounced the ban on the Moroccan independence movement Istaqlal,[230] and saw the arrest of the Sultan as an act of criminal folly, since the Sultan was the only possible spokesman for his country in any eventual negotiations.[231]

His attention turned next to Tunisia, a second flash-point in France's North African troubles. Again he insisted that negotiations in view of independence were inevitable, and that in this case the obvious representative of the Tunisians was Bourguiba.[232] As for the government's policies in that other crumbling outpost of empire, Indochina, he denounced them as 'le mal absolu'.[233] The outcome of his involvement in these issues was the final extinction of any remaining spark of faith in the M.R.P., whose leaders occupied the key ministerial posts during much of this period, and in the Fourth Republic generally. The M.R.P., he declared in December 1953, had betrayed its Christian mission. It was 'le complice le plus efficace de

Mammon', playing into the hands of the right-wing factions that clung to their business interests in the Orient or, more sinisterly, dreamed of secession in North Africa.[234] 'Jusqu'à la tuerie de Casablanca de décembre 1952,' he said, 'j'ai soutenu contre vents et marées ces chefs dont le comportement était odieux. Mais je leur trouvais des excuses parce que je ne voulais pas renoncer à mon espérance . . .'[235] And on the fall of Dien-Bien-Phu which signalled the end of the Indochinese war as far as France was concerned, a bloody and disastrous end to a hopeless campaign, he declared his total disillusionment: the party which had so raised his hopes in the months after the Liberation, had failed, and Christian democracy, in its practical results, had shown itself no more successful than integral nationalism.[236] From this moment, he attacked relentlessly the leaders of the party. They were power-seekers, he wrote, pursuing right-wing policies that created a great gulf between them and their Christian principles.[237]

From the time of his switching his 'Bloc-notes' to L'Express, his attacks on the regime became more and more uncompromising. In his first piece for the paper, he wrote: 'Chaque Français voit qu'il n'y a plus d'État et que sa patrie est au moment d'en mourir.'[238] He was, of course, unfair: he kept almost total silence on the very real economic achievements of the Fourth Republic, except for a grudging comment that 'Jamais mauvaise politique n'aura donné de meilleures finances'.[239] His endless compilation of the regime's shortcomings—its alleged neglect of social problems like alcoholism, its refusal to instigate fiscal or constitutional reform, its unreadiness for the unexpected, its ministerial instability, above all its colonial policies—probably, in its effect on public opinion, helped the Republic to its grave.

He reserved special scorn for the governments of Laniel, Faure, Bourgès-Maunoury and, especially, the Socialist Guy Mollet. Mollet, he believed, had led the moderate Left—which, like the M.R.P., had promised so much ten years earlier—in the footsteps of the Christian democrats: he had implemented policies favourable to the hated Right.[240] His role in the 'diplomatic Dien-Bien-Phu' of Suez[241] and his mishandling of the greatest crisis of them all—Algeria—gave him a special place in Mauriac's demonology. He seemed to epitomise that lack of control over events that was the constant impression given by Fourth Republican governments; and never more so than at the time of the scandalous bombing of Sakiet, carried out on the orders of French generals who had not even bothered to consult the prime minister.[242]

The only politician of the Fourth Republic for whom Mauriac had a profound and lasting respect was Pierre Mendès-France. It is a telling comment on his estimation of the Christian democrats that he, a leader among Catholic intellectuals, should now support a Radical, heir to Ferry and Combes in party allegiance if not in every aspect of his beliefs. 'D'une autre espèce que les carpes du Palais-Bourbon',[243] Mendès manifested an independence and courage which won him Mauriac's support as early as 1953.[244] The latter saw in his outlook moral principles that were more in keeping with true Christian values than were the attitudes of the M.R.P.[245] His diagnosis of Mendès' fall from office after a mere seven months in power was that intelligence and integrity had been sabotaged by inferior minds that distrusted such qualities.[246]

The true significance of Mauriac's support for Mendès-France is that it revealed that the period in his life when he had been willing to support a party, a team of men operating within a sovereign parliamentary system, was almost over. What Alexander Werth, with only slight exaggeration, calls Mauriac's 'reverence, hero-worship and adoration' of Mendès, his acceptance of him 'almost mystically, as a providential figure',[247] was a clear sign that Mauriac was moving back to an élitist position, to a preparedness to support the brilliant individual, the strong man who might turn the nation's steps into a more honourable direction. Mendès-France's fall was a bitter disappointment, but there was still one man, the most outstanding individual of all, who now returned to the centre of Mauriac's political world and who remained there for the rest of Mauriac's life.

Chapter Four

MAURIAC UNDER DE GAULLE

(i) *Rediscovery of a hero*

Between the wars, Mauriac had consistently expressed his scorn of parliamentary democracy, at least in the form in which it had functioned (or, he would have said, ceased to function) under the Third Republic. He had come to revise this view because he had seen how, in the case not only of Maurras but of many conservatives, often Catholic conservatives, it was prone to develop into an admiration for 'efficient' but liberty-denying Fascist dictatorship; and from there it was but a short step, as events had proved, to a tragic alliance of so-called patriots with the deadliest enemies of their country. In the post-Liberation period he had hoped in all sincerity that the parliamentary mode of government would work, and although he warned as early as 1946 that the Fourth Republic had not resolved all of the weaknesses in the system inherited from the Third,[1] he went on doggedly insisting that government by an elected assembly was 'la seule forme de gouvernement compatible avec la liberté individuelle', and that it must be made to succeed.[2] This hope, like so many others, was shattered by his increasing frustration during the 1950s. In the politicians who endlessly replaced each other at the helm of government only to prove no more able than their predecessors to cope with France's problems, especially in the realm of colonial affairs, he saw none of the qualities which were for him the mark of a great statesman. 'L'homme d'État digne de ce nom', he declared,

> est celui qui fait prévaloir ses desseins sur les passions d'un Parlement, comme il saurait, s'il était dictateur et maître absolu, réduire au silence ses propres passions. Tel est le don de persuader et de dominer qui n'a été départi à aucun de nos chefs débiles,

mais qu'il ne faut jamais désespérer de découvrir un jour dans un homme nouveau.[3]

It looked for a while as though Mendès-France could be that new man, but with his defeat in 1955 there remained only one figure to turn to in the hope of strong and worthy government. The seeds of Mauriac's renewed support of de Gaulle had been sown the previous year when he attended one of the General's press conferences (for the first time in many years, testifies Claude Mauriac[4]). His admiration for the lucidity with which de Gaulle analysed the current French and world situations—as uncompromising as Bossuet, it seemed to Mauriac, in his reminder of the collective tomb prepared for all mankind by the makers of the hydrogen bomb—was expressed publicly the next day, April 8th, 1954. The error of the R.P.F. now lay behind de Gaulle, he said. The General had survived that phase and his authority stood intact. But whether this prestige could or even should be translated into executive power, Mauriac was not sure. De Gaulle could justly claim to incarnate France; but that, in a way, was the trouble: his scorn of opposing views meant that the spectre of dictatorship dogged the General's footsteps. He dwarfed the politicians of the Fourth Republic but perhaps their mediocrity was the price France had to pay for her liberty.[5]

What finally put an end to Mauriac's attempts to convince himself of the virtues of parliamentary democracy was the fall of Mendès-France. That the party system had not accommodated de Gaulle in the two years after the war was not surprising: the General's own inflexible character was no small factor in the malfunctioning of the machine of government at that time. But that Mendès, a parliamentarian who accepted the rules of the game, should be rejected in spite of the palpable successes of his brief ministry, was the final proof, for Mauriac, of de Gaulle's analysis of democracy in France. 'La démonstration est faite', he wrote, 'et donne raison au général de Gaulle: le régime des partis, tel que nous le pratiquons en France, est destructeur de tout gouvernement.'[6] And yet, what of the alternatives? What of a presidential system on American lines? Mauriac saw this as likely to be exploited by the Right or by the Communists, with the struggle to win the presidency between the representatives of the two blocs liable to lead to nothing short of civil war. Unless, of course, the president were to be de Gaulle himself, the one man capable of ending the Algerian troubles by the creation of a North African federation of free states.[7] But on the whole, Mauriac set no great store by constitutional change. Such a reform would be too lengthy a process in any case, and action was needed immediately.[8] So what mattered was the character of the head of government, not whether his office bore the title of president or prime minister.

That man, Mauriac was fully convinced as 1956 dawned, must be Charles de Gaulle. The humiliation of Mollet at the hands of the Algiers mob in February of that year, and the national humiliation of Suez—not just the shame of military suppression of a weak opponent but also that of suspending the operation at the behest of Britain, herself the puppet of America—confirmed him in this view. 'Vers qui crierons-nous?' he asked in despair;

> Quel nom nous hante sinon celui de l'homme qui, au temps où la patrie était piétinée, profanée par la présence ennemie, demeura seul à Londres et, face aux États-Unis et à l'Empire britannique, maintint la vieille nation souveraine quoique captive, indépendante quoique esclave, rayonnante au sein du pire désastre qu'elle ait jamais subi? De Gaulle! De Gaulle![9]

However, as he recognised a few days later, the problem of how to reconcile de Gaulle's leadership with a form of regime to which the General was implacably opposed remained to be solved.[10] Mauriac was still reluctant to see supreme power, without proper checks and balances, put into the hands of one man. But as 1957 rolled by, with no sign of a halt to the ever-escalating Algerian crisis, he declared that de Gaulle's return, with all the risks it entailed, was now the only alternative to rapid national disintegration.[11]

Within a few months, political events caught up with Mauriac's conjectures. On the 13th of May, 1958, and during the days that followed he reflected that the circumstances of de Gaulle's return, which now looked certain, were far from those which he had envisaged. His first fear, in view of Salan's famous call of 'Vive de Gaulle!' from the balcony of the Algiers Hôtel de Ville, was that the General would be merely a puppet of the other generals, an agent of the militarist Right, hanging on to a French Algeria at the cost of unimaginable bloodshed. De Gaulle must remember the role that had been his since 1940: servant of the nation, the whole nation.[12] In a further public self-analysis he asked whether he was going to oppose the General's return after so many months of campaigning for it; and he adumbrated the conditions under which he was willing to suspend what was left of his belief in parliamentary democracy and support de Gaulle's authoritarian presence in the seat of government:

Si le général de Gaulle nous montre 'comment faire
autrement', si les Français et le peuple algérien se réconcilient
sous son égide, dans une Algérie autonome où les deux drapeaux
flotteront et ne seront jamais plus séparés, eh bien, je me
consolerai de voir la République devenir autoritaire, j'accepterai
que Marianne ait tout à coup cette grande gueule, ce grand style,
cette puissance d'orgueil, d'indifférence et de mépris, dont on
peut s'offenser . . . mais quoi? Quand le général de Gaulle parlera
en Europe au nom de la France, ce sera fini pour elle d'être
humiliée. Quel soulagement . . .
    Je mesure le risque. S'il ne dépendait que de moi,
j'accepterais de le courir.[13]

This article suggests that Mauriac's mind was already made up by
this date, that the prospect of peace in Algeria and, perhaps even more
enticing, of a loud French voice in Europe and in the world, had
swayed him rather easily away from the democratic principles he had
earlier supported. And, indeed, there now began a period in which he
was obliged to defend himself against his former colleagues of the
Centre and Centre-Left, who accused him of betraying his principles.
The evidence indicates, however, that he had not yet fully reconciled
himself to what he feared would be the autocratic rule of de Gaulle, or
perhaps that he had not fully grasped the implications of his support
for the General. For he tended initially to regard de Gaulle's regime as
an interim one, after which a new and unified left-wing party, having
buried the hatchet with which Socialists and Communists had for so
long chopped at each other, would assume power, led perhaps by
Mitterrand, Mendès or Defferre.[14] 'De Gaulle ne peut avoir d'autre
héritier,' he insisted, 'que l'État démocratique restauré.'[15] Furthermore, although expressing total faith in de Gaulle's motives, he ex-
perienced doubts as to his strategy and disappointment that he did not
say more to placate the Algerian Moslems.[16] When the September
constitutional referendum drew near, Mauriac advised his readers to
vote 'Yes', but with some reservations. To support de Gaulle, he
thought, was to gamble on the unpredictable, but it was the best
chance of avoiding civil war. He added that whatever the result of the
referendum his own long-term sympathies would still remain with the
Left.[17] And when the news came of de Gaulle's spectacular success in
the referendum, he declared his delight that the General had apparently won the support of both Left and Right. Thus the fear that he
might be a mere figurehead of reaction was dispelled. Mauriac ad-

mitted the wrongness of his earlier misgivings on this score, and, in the longer perspective, his error at ever having turned away from the man who was still, as in 1944, 'le premier des nôtres'.[18]

(ii) *Gaullist myth-maker*

Between the autumn of 1958 and his death in 1970, the only doubt expressed by Mauriac as to the wisdom and rightness of any word or deed on the part of de Gaulle concerned the latter's personal visit to Franco in the last summer of Mauriac's (and de Gaulle's) life; and even then, he was willing to believe that de Gaulle had justifiable reasons for wishing to see the old Spanish anti-Christ.[19] De Gaulle, by that time, had of course retired; during the eleven years of his tenure of the presidency of the Fifth Republic, Mauriac voiced not a single disagreement of opinion with him. He became the established press champion of de Gaulle, the unofficial *historiographe du roi*, the defender whose ecstatic eulogies of the master did not stop short, in many people's eyes, of sycophancy. The regular *bloc-note* was still his vehicle, but it proved impossible to continue publishing it in *L'Express*, so totally did Mauriac's view of the regime differ from that of the radical newspaper. In April 1961, the precise point of a long-expected rupture being the paper's stand against de Gaulle's Algerian policy, Mauriac ended his seven-year association with *L'Express* and published his column henceforth in *Le Figaro littéraire*. It was an acrimonious parting, and in its wake there trailed a long exchange of jibes between Mauriac and the editor of *L'Express*, Jean-Jacques Servan-Schreiber, whom Mauriac, on account of the whizz-kid reputation he enjoyed in the early 1960s, rechristened 'Kennedillon'.[20]

Mauriac undoubtedly relished the press warfare in which he found himself almost permanently engaged from the date of de Gaulle's return. This, for him, was an opportunity to lambast the party politicians who had caused him such frustration when they were in power, and whose vulnerability, now that they had so comprehensively lost it, he was quick to exploit. The parties, he wrote, were the cold and bloodless extremities of the body politic. De Gaulle, in setting up his direct relationship with the French people through the device of the referendum and, later, the direct popular election of himself as president, had not so much destroyed them as simply stepped into the void they had left.[21] They were now cast out to the margin of politics, futile bystanders to the great contractual *rapport* between the true poles of sovereignty, de Gaulle and the people.[22] Mauriac took such joy, in fact, in ridiculing the parties that even when they were no longer in a position to offend him as they had offended him before 1958, he could not resist a regular retrospective summary of their inglorious 'achievements'. His readers, well into the 1960s, were entertained, when they were not bored, by gleeful accounts of the politicians' *coups*: the arrest of the Sultan of Morocco or of Ben-Bella,[23] their successes in Indochina and in getting rid of Pierre Mendès-France.[24] By such methods, Mauriac hoped that the discredit into which the Fourth Republic had fallen by May, 1958, would remain permanent. For he had now withdrawn his commitment to an eventual non-Gaullist future in which the Left or the M.R.P. might be given a second chance. A return to the days of impotent parliamentary government would be fatal for France, he now insisted, and, 'tout républicains, tout démocrates que nous sommes', had to be opposed as a retrograde step.[25] He scornfuly imagined the regime of a President Mitterrand, puppet of London, overseer of a weak, unauthoritative minority government.[26] The prospect was too appalling, and in September, 1960, he finally abandoned his view of the Gaullist 'interregnum',[27] having already announced some months before his 'consent' to live under the Gaullist regime until the end of his days.[28]

He reacted fiercely to accusations of having betrayed his former democratic faith. Between 1958 and 1960 he could retort plausibly that de Gaulle was the only alternative to a power struggle—probably an armed one—between the Fascist Right and a resurgent Popular Front, and that his presence was the best guarantee of an eventual return to democratic normality.[29] But gradually he shifted his ground, arguing that de Gaulle's regime was itself democratic. France had needed a new form of democracy, the parliamentary form having failed. 'La démocratie se confond pour vous,' he told his opponents,

> avec le parlementarisme à la française, dont nous avons été à
> deux doigts de périr: cette paralysie de l'exécutif par le législatif,
> qui a fait de nous la risée du monde, c'est cela à vos yeux le signe
> d'un régime républicain authenthique.[30]

But de Gaulle's 'consular' Republic was equally legitimate, he argued, and a good deal more effective. 'Démocrate, je ne suis pas le moins du monde gêné', he admitted, 'par un régime consulaire.'[31] And as de Gaulle's plan for direct presidential elections unfurled, Mauriac became its fervent champion: what more democratic system could be imagined than one in which the head of state and government remains dependent on the people's direct support, accepted or rejected by them through the ballot-box or plebiscite?[32] To the accusation that de Gaulle was a new Bonaparte, Mauriac likewise had his ready riposte. The crucial difference lay in motive, the Bonapartes seeking personal glory, de Gaulle seeking only to enhance the glory of Mother France. 'Les Bonaparte se servaient de la France, de Gaulle la sert', he wrote in 1959,[33] and repeated the same idea over and over again until the referendum of 1962, approving de Gaulle's project for presidential elections, seemed to Mauriac to close the issue of how democratic or undemocratic the Fifth Republic was.

On precise issues, the history of Mauriac's opinions during these years merges totally with that of de Gaulle's policies, and needs only be related very briefly. On the immediate problem, Algeria, he supported de Gaulle's solution entirely, and engaged with considerable courage in a series of verbal attacks on the 'égorgeurs' of the O.A.S.,[34] in whom he saw the descendants of the old anti-Dreyfus forces, opponents of liberty and the Rights of Man,[35] latter-day embodiments of the 'eternal' extreme Right.[36] De Gaulle's policy of independence from the Anglo-Saxon 'hegemony' likewise had Mauriac's gushing support. He expressed his delight that France no longer 'danced around the Pentagon', hand in hand with Britain.[37] Britain and the U.S.A. were as inseparable as ever in Mauriac's imagination: the visit of Eisenhower to Paris in 1958 gave him the chance to remind his readers not only of American inperialism but also of British perfidy on familiar historical occasions.[38] De Gaulle's veto of British membership of the E.E.C. was warmly applauded by him,[39] as was the General's cold indifference to the prospect of a federal Europe—in any case, said Mauriac, German and British nationalism would always prevent the realisation of such a goal.[40]

His contribution to the debates on these and other issues was of minimal importance, his subservience to de Gaulle effacing any chance of original comment. More interesting was his emergence in a role ideally suited to his literary gifts, that of creator of images of the man de Gaulle. His taste in this respect was not infallible, to be sure: many a reader must have been amused, rather than moved, by the romanticised images of de Gaulle as a legendary knight in enchanted armour, the arrows of his enemies rebounding from his breastplate[41]; or de Gaulle as a hunted stag leaping into a pool (symbol of the profundity of the French people's love) as the dogs move in[42]; or de Gaulle as a solitary chieftain oblivious of the barking of the two rival packs

(O.A.S. and Communists) at his heels[43]; or as a lion-tamer in the middle of a cage of roaring beasts[44]; or as a great druidic oak, unmoved by the tempests.[45] When he avoided such graphic excesses, however, Mauriac could encapsulate more plausibly the heroic mission of his master, bring out the grandeur of de Gaulle's struggle, stress 'le tragique d'une Histoire suspendue à la fragile vie d'un seul homme'.[46] His principal device was that of his beloved paradox, and he exploited it to underline the heroism of this one, lonely man who had taken the collective destinies of Frenchmen on his shoulders, 'cet homme très fort et pourtant très faible, qui a toute la France dans la pensée et dans le cœur et qui pourtant est seul . . .'.[47] De Gaulle's solitude is a recurring theme, especially in the period up to 1962, those years of consolidation of his regime. Psychologically, Mauriac needed to close his eyes to the existence of the General's highly proficient inner circle of aides and to the ever more powerful machinery of state that made him less and less vulnerable to criticism. He needed to cling to his image of de Gaulle as a lonely man, and of himself as a lone supporter, uniting his 'obscure solitude' to the 'illustre solitude' of his chief.[48] He had always sided with the underdog, and in this period of transition, before his role was transformed into that of defender of the establishment, it clearly comforted and uplifted him to see himself, along with de Gaulle, in a minority camp once again, a minority of two held upright only by their unassailable belief that they were right. His closeness in age to de Gaulle was an important factor also. He could present the General and himself as two wise old men who knew better than their turbulent juniors the road the nation had to follow. 'Ma sénilité a vu plus clair que votre maturité,' he told Simone de Beauvoir, delightfully. 'Les 70 hivers que je comptais (. . .) ont été moins aveugles que vos 50 printemps.'[49] Age gave Mauriac an aloofness, a long perspective on men and events. It was a symbol of political wisdom, not only of individuals but of nations: behind de Gaulle, silent but strong, lay the self-preserving instincts of the 'vieux peuple' —'ce vieux peuple qui ne sait pas ce qu'il veut, mais qui sait fort bien ce qu'il ne veut pas'.[50] The successful result of the 1962 referendum, Mauriac wrote, confirmed his faith in 'ce vieux pays dont l'éducation politique (. . .) a atteint une maturité dont le monde entier a été frappé'.[51]

He was of course aware of the element of mythification in his imagery. But he also knew that myth was an important factor in de Gaulle's hold on power. 'Il incarne la France de l'Histoire,' he said.

'De Gaulle est le cerveau et le cœur d'une grande nation rassemblée, d'une grande nation une et indivisible, *qui n'existe pas . . .*'[52] And at the heart of the myth, lay de Gaulle's 'certaine idée de la France', which Mauriac declared that he shared in all its details and which he defined as 'cette nostalgie d'une grandeur encore à notre portée malgré tant d'erreurs'.[53] That de Gaulle should exist at this particular historic moment, to save the nation from the abyss and restore it to greatness, not once but twice, Mauriac saw as a sign of God's love for the ancient people of France.[54] De Gaulle, quite literally 'l'homme providentiel', had been sent by God (or Destiny, Mauriac added, so as not to deter his infidel readers, whose votes were equally valid) in order to guide France.[55] How far the General himself was conscious of his divinely inspired mission was a matter that he did not probe too deeply. He liked to present de Gaulle as a master pragmatist, 'le plus grand réaliste et peut-être le seul réaliste de la politique française',[56] characterised by a 'fidélité au réel',[57] a 'soumission au réel'.[58] But, mindful of the association, in Maurrassian days, of realism and amorality, he reminded his public that de Gaulle was a practising Christian[59] and that, though it would be naïve to imagine that his actions were based on the commands of Holy Scripture, his policies had produced results, directly or indirectly, that all Christians could applaud.[60]

Whatever may be thought of the quality of argument that he brought to his defence of the General, the supreme mastery of polemical technique which Mauriac had acquired by this time can hardly be gainsaid. Because of the variety of tone and mode of address to the reader, his *bloc-notes*, even when, in the 1960s, their content became repetitive, will long repay reading. When the gravity of the situation demanded it, Mauriac could assume the resounding tone of a Bossuet and deliver his message in pulpit-style oratory. In March 1962, when an O.A.S. commando unit massacred a group of school-teachers and social workers at El Biar in Algeria, he summoned sympathy for the victims and the promise of vengeance against their murderers. 'Ô frères,' he wrote,

> êtes-vous de leur côté, ou avec ceux qu'ils ont abattus?
> Continuerez-vous d'hésiter entre les instituteurs et leurs assassins?
> Entre ceux qui torturent et ceux qui instruisent, et qui ont été
> souvent et qui restent souvent des officiers et des soldats?[61]

Or else he would volley a direct address at his enemies, often in mocking tones. In the following example, which contains a rare instance of the adjective 'vieux' being given pejorative value, he ends

in a paroxysm of scorn against the party politicians and enemies of de
Gaulle:

> Vous ne le haïssez que parce qu'il aura été plus intelligent
> au sens absolu, en face de vos yeux crevés, de vos oreilles
> bouchées, et qu'il aura eu raison, contre vous tous, vieille droite
> et vieille gauche, vieux maurrassiens et vieux radicaux, vieux
> socialistes et vieux communistes, tous pareils au fond, tous
> confits dans le même vinaigre et dans le même bocal.[62]

The dividing line between telling satire and excessive denigration
was a narrow one in Mauriac's polemic, as this example shows. In
1962, during a period of extreme stress following the latest attempt on
de Gaulle's life, he rediscovered all the venom which, as the young
novelist of *Préséances*, he had employed against the Fils des grandes
maisons. Recalling the 'ancien vomissement' of the Fourth Republic,
he reflected scornfully on the prospects for France if de Gaulle were to
die: a reprieve for '(les) chômeurs du système (. . .), les dents un peu
plus longues, de la bave aux commissures. Et tout rentrera au sérail
dans le désordre accoutumé.'[63] He dismissed Monnerville, the president of the Senate, as a man whom nobody had heard of but who had
now gone down in history, made an immortal name for himself, by
his opposition to de Gaulle.[64] And in the case of Georges Bidault, one-
time Resistance colleague and fellow-Christian democrat, he was not
above petty caricature of the man's smallness of stature, physical as
well as intellectual, compared with that of the towering de Gaulle.[65]

He was capable, more often, of more pleasing effects. His urge
for paradox stood him in good stead. He could mock the futility of
adversaries whose actions seemed impeccably designed to produce the
reverse of the intended result.[66] He could reflect that if France's most
stable republican regime ever continued to attack the greatest barrage
of criticism, then this must prove something about the mentality of
the detractors.[67] He would switch his ground disconcertingly. At one
moment, he assumed the guise of the erudite historian, drawing impressive historical parallels; or else he found an apt literary analogy,
often to devastatingly witty effect. 'Pascal a écrit la prière pour le bon
usage des maladies,' he wrote. 'De Gaulle nous aura appris le bon
usage du parlement.'[68] But at other times he would feign to be a
simple soul, a layman adrift in the technicalities of politics, and invite
ordinary readers to identify with him rather than with the intellectual
heavy-weights, Sartre or Servan-Schreiber.[69] And like Pascal, the
Pascal of the *Provinciales*, he would infuriate irreconcilable enemies by

refusing to see any difference between them. 'Quand il s'agit de de Gaulle,' he remarked, 'la gauche la plus intelligente ne pèse pas mieux ses mots que la droite la plus bête: la même rage enfante la même déraison.'[70] 'Les frères ennemis', he said of Left and Right, 'restent des frères et ils se ressemblent.'[71] Another favourite technique was what he called 'prêter le flanc à la moquerie'[72]—disarming his opponent by warmly agreeing with his most outrageous accusations. That he confused de Gaulle with Joan of Arc, or even mistook him for Christ, were long-standing jokes in the opposition press. But Mauriac met them head on: 'Eh bien, oui! Cet homme est entré dans la compagnie des héros et des saints qui, à travers le temps et ses malheurs, ont maintenu la France vivante.'[73] Or: 'On va protester que j'assimile de Gaulle au Christ. Ce ne serait certes pas un blasphème. . . .'[74] He took constant delight in predicting the 'I always said so!' response of his adversaries, and he would provoke such responses by tongue-in-cheek avowals of lifelong monarchist sympathies.[75]

By the late 1960s Mauriac was revelling in his situation. One thing, to be sure, was lacking: namely, a personal sign of de Gaulle's favour. The General, who never found it easy to express gratitude, did not encourage intimacy on a personal level. The comment by Mauriac's second son Jean, in response to de Gaulle's warm tributes to Mauriac after the latter's death, hints at an unfulfilled dream of his father's: 'Que le général de Gaulle n'a-t-il dit cela à François Mauriac vivant!'[76] Still, Mauriac, as the journalist who had steadfastly supported him for so many years, shared in de Gaulle's triumph. Being 'du côté de la manche' in politics was a new experience for him, one he increasingly enjoyed. He could not know that the shock of 1968 was just around the corner.

(iii) *The last of the mammoths*

In 1966 and 1967 the quality of Mauriac's journalism fell to what was probably its lowest level. He had grown wearyingly prone to self-quotation in his gleeful assertions of Fifth Republican France's independence from America, of her renewed prestige, especially in the eyes of the Third World, as a teacher of spiritual values, and of the seemingly permanent restoration by de Gaulle of order and stability at home. He no longer responded to the daily events of the political scene, but preferred, through old age or mere complacency, a more refracted role, reacting to the barbs of the opposition press. He could only survive as a journalist if he had enemies with whom to exchange broadsides; and, failing to see any other challenge to the Gaullist regime, he perhaps deliberately exaggerated the importance of press criticism of de Gaulle, the more to appreciate his own value as a defender of the man and his system. Like the Gaullist hierarchy itself, Mauriac seriously misread the state of the nation at this time and failed to anticipate from which direction a major challenge might come, or even to realise that the situation was less stable than it seemed on the surface. De Gaulle had achieved all that was humanly possible;[77] for the first time in sixty years, Mauriac deemed himself 'gouverné raisonnablement'.[78] How could anyone seek to overthrow such a regime, or fail to bow before 'le ton (. . .) et le style de celui qui parle en notre nom?[79] He could even permit himself a happy fantasy on the vexed question of the succession:

> Après de Gaulle . . . Après de Gaulle. . . . Ils en sont tous
> obsédés, les amis et les ennemis. Et s'il n'y avait pas d'après
> de Gaulle? . . . J'ai fait le rêve que l'homme massif et comme
> pétrifié, debout à la barre, ne changerait plus. Il serait là, pareil à
> lui-même, recevant chaque jour à l'Élysée les adorateurs d'un
> roi-mage africain, et tous les six mois, à l'occasion de la
> conférence de presse rituelle, l'hommage des journalistes du
> monde entier. L'histoire, chaque jour, confirmerait la sagesse de
> sa politique: tout se déroulerait selon ses vues, sans qu'il ait rien à
> faire d'autre que d'être là . . .[80]

Mauriac had long recognised the existence of two Frances: the actual France of citizens in their socio-economic context and the vision of an eternal France that was the 'certaine idée' of de Gaulle. 'Les Français', he once wrote, 'ne l'auront à aucun moment détourné de la France.'[81] Yet he did not appreciate that the division between France and the French was a potentially explosive one. He was increasingly intolerant of opponents of the General, of those who preferred their concept of modern France to his, seeing them as enemies of the state and of legitimacy. He even doubted whether they should have access to French television as a vehicle for their anti-Gaullist and therefore anti-French views.[82] Clearly, Mauriac was now unable or unwilling to understand the opposition's point of view.

The *événements* of May, 1968, and the resultant acceleration of events towards de Gaulle's final withdrawal from the political scene came as a traumatic shock to Mauriac, one which probably even lessened his will to live. He was at Malagar, preoccupied with the writing of *Un adolescent d'autrefois*, his first novel for some fifteen years, when the first signs of trouble appeared. His initial comment was published on May 5th, and was a somewhat ungracious comparison between the students of 1968 and those who had campaigned for justice in the Dreyfus battles so many decades earlier. He saw as yet no menace to the regime in what was happening, and dismissed the students' uprising as a movement of romantic adolescents seeking action for its own sake before the responsibilities of adult life caught up with them, and using Mao, Castro, Che Guevara and the Vietcong as triggers for the release of their energies. The revolt, he said, bore no relevance to the problems of France.[83]

Once back in Paris, his view changed very rapidly. He saw the possibility of an escalation of the conflict into a revolution of great consequence, and when the Minister of Education, Peyrefitte, denounced the 'fanaticism and violence' of the students, Mauriac was one of five Nobel Prize winners to sign a petition of protest to de Gaulle. The heavy-handed reaction of the Minister, especially the closing of the Sorbonne which resulted not in a stifling of the revolt but merely in its displacement to the potentially more dangerous arena of the streets, was criticised by Mauriac, in his *bloc-note* of May 11th, as a serious error.[84]

By early June, however, he was praising the old master de Gaulle for the apparent success of his handling of the crisis and for the political wisdom he had once again shown in his decision to call fresh elections.[85] But Mauriac had been hurt. Even the resounding Gaullist success in the elections, giving them a bigger majority than before, brought him no comfort. The damage had been done, he wrote in articles of June 23rd and 24th. The children had played with fire, and the brief but damaging conflagration had destroyed the fruits of ten years of order and peace.[86] He was especially offended that such a blow should have been dealt, in international eyes, to the image of a united France at this precise moment, when the choice of Paris as the venue of the Vietnam peace talks had bestowed such an honour on the nation, acknowledging her place in the centre of world affairs.[87]

But at least de Gaulle was still there, the old Sisyphus constantly rolling the rock of state uphill and retrieving it indefatigably when lesser mortals reversed its upward path.[88] The decision of de Gaulle to stake all on a last referendum, therefore, struck Mauriac as surprising and alarming. 'Cette fois', he told the General publicly through the medium of his *bloc-notes*, 'je n'aurai pas compris les raisons de votre politique. On n'a jamais vu personne se suicider en plein bonheur.'[89]

What his immediate reactions were to the 'No' vote in the referendum are not recorded, because on the day when he himself went to cast his vote in favour, Sunday, April 27th, 1969, Mauriac suffered a fall and sustained a broken shoulder which prevented him from writing for some weeks. When he eventually ended this enforced silence, in a published interview with a fellow journalist on *Le Figaro littéraire*, he remarked philosophically that de Gaulle had no doubt had his personal reasons for his action. But as for France, she was now threatened by a return to the chaos from which de Gaulle had protected her for so long. 'C'est donc pour la France que je souffre', he said, 'plus que pour de Gaulle.'[90]

And suffer Mauriac did, for France, and for his own shattered Gaullist dream, during the final months of his life. The future, like all futures, would be the work of the present-day young generation, and its revolt against de Gaulle's order persuaded Mauriac that the road that lay ahead for his country would be drastically and terrifyingly different from that which he had fondly and confidently imagined. The gulf between himself and modern youth, which he lamented in a series of *bloc-notes* in June and July, 1968, resolved itself, he thought, into a question of historical perspective and sensitivity. Young students lacked the sense not just of pride but even of interest in the past of their nation—that past that was the bedrock of faith in a Gaullist future. '"Comment voulez-vous que je m'intéresse à ces histoires, moi qui suis né en 1945?"' he imagined the young man of 1968 saying, and he associated this lack of awareness of the national heritage with other allegedly dehumanising factors in modern culture, the *nouveau roman* and abstract art, two of his *bêtes noires* in the last period of his life. 'Cette génération sans mémoire', he wrote, 'c'est celle du roman sans personnages, de la peinture sans visage.'[91] He had once described men of his age, born in the nineteenth century and intellectually formed by those nationalist writers who were determined to see France rise again from the defeat of 1870, as the 'last mammoths', wandering and disorientated in an alien epoch.[92] And now the ice age seemed to be upon him. It was time to go, to pass into history. His advanced age, so recently a sign of superiority, was now a portent of redundancy. What place was there for him in a world dominated by the ideas of Hegel, Marx, Freud and Marcuse?[93] —an age which had succeeded, when that of Émile Combes had failed, in finally killing the idea of a Christian God.[94]

Mauriac continued to write his *bloc-notes* until he was overtaken by the final weakness that led to his death in September 1970. But he wrote less and less frequently on political issues. He felt, in depths of bitter despair, that there was nothing left to say, nobody left to listen to him. He wrote on June 9th, 1968, that he had tried three times to compose an article giving his considered view of the *événements*. But, he said, 'j'y renonce définitivement:

'devant cette révolution de la jeunesse, comment ne me sentirais-je pas, à mon âge, plus éloigné d'elle qu'un Martien? (. . .) Peut-être aurais-je su lui dire ce que d'autres ne lui ont pas dit. Je n'en ai plus la force, ni peut-être le courage. Je n'écrirai donc pas le 'J'accuse' auquel j'avais songé et me résigne à donner les notes rédigées après le discours du 30 mai (de Gaulle's announcement of a referendum) . . . et qui n'ont plus d'intérêt pour personne.'[95]

He turned to another subject, to the currents of new ideas within the Church. Here too the old Modernist, erstwhile defender of the Sillon and, in the 1950s, of the worker priests, now showed a deep conservatism, a suspicion of change. The so-called crisis of authority in the Church alarmed him. He sprang to the defence of orthodoxy on issues like contraception and the celibacy of the priesthood.[96] Change, change for the sake of change, he saw as productive of disintegration.[97] Revolt was an instinct of youth: Rimbaud represented the archetype both of youth and of iconoclasm. But the modern Rimbauds should not imagine, he said, that their revolt would benefit them.[98] Revolution, whether in Russia, France or elsewhere, had no power to transform men's lives for the better, to give them liberty or improve their lot.[99] Stability and order were the basis of individual as well as collective happiness, and they were assured only by an authoritarian state. 'En vérité,' he proclaimed,

je me sens tout entier, et passionnément, du côté de l'État, non pas du tout parce que je suis né bourgeois, mais parce que je ne doute pas que le plus grand malheur pour un peuple c'est qu'il n'ait plus d'État . . .'[100]

A last glimmer of hope, on the political level, was afforded by the apparent resilience of Gaullist institutions. De Gaulle had provided for the future of a strongly-led state by the institution of the popularly-elected president. All depended, of course, on the quality of the man in power. Had Mauriac lived into the era of President Giscard d'Estaing, whom he constantly regarded as a shallow political adventurer,[101] his reactions would have made fascinating reading. But

Pompidou was at the helm, a man whom, on one celebrated occasion, he had ambiguously characterised as 'Raminagrobis',[102] but for whom, from the time of the *événements*, he had a growing admiration.[103] The presence of such men, overriding and overruling the turbulent mob of would-be revolutionaries, career-builders and professional parliamentary 'talkers', ensured that France's future would be in accordance with her true destiny. This destiny, he declared in what was virtually his last comment on French politics, was properly a monarchist one. Not that there need be a crowned king; nor that the interests of France should be identified with those of one family, one dynasty, as the Bonapartes had tried to identify it. 'Mais le désir d'être gouverné par quelqu'un, ce pays l'a toujours ressenti, et c'est la clef de toutes ses aventures et mésaventures politiques.'[104]

Events—*the* events—had pushed Mauriac to a lucid acceptance of where he stood in politics. He stood, as deep in his private conscience he had always stood, on the side of tradition, authority and order. This was an attitude he had tried to renounce for two main reasons. Firstly, he feared it had been ingrained into him by virtue of birth and environment, whereas he wished to exercise his own judgment, choose his options for himself; there is a strong parallel in this respect between his politics and his religion, which he also regarded as part of his social and family heritage, but which he had come fully to embrace of himself. And secondly, the example lay before him, throughout his lifetime, of apostles of order who had connived at violence, defenders of the nation who had collaborated with the enemy. It was the example of Maurras, in particular, that made Mauriac wish to be of the Left. But his love of de Gaulle and, through de Gaulle, of the traditions of France finally revealed Mauriac to himself and to the world as an instinctively authoritarian nationalist. But he was also a Christian; and that is why one must ask about Mauriac, as he so often asked about Maurras and Barrès, what the relationship was, in this complex and many-sided man, between his patriotism and his religion, between his moral and his political beliefs. This question must be the central concern of the concluding chapter of this study.

Chapter Five

MAURIAC, CHRISTIAN AND PATRIOT

Various attacks have been made on Mauriac's political position. He has been accused of cultivating his career as a political commentator for low motives. It had been said, for example, that he was merely seeking to retain an audience when his literary vein was all but exhausted, and that he wanted to establish a base for his personal vendettas.[1] This second point has been reinforced by doubts in many quarters about Mauriac's ability to reconcile Christian charity with his angry exclamations, his harsh judgments, his violent denunciations, his often petty feuds. Even the largely sympathetic Xavier Grall writes that although Mauriac preached charity to politicians he was scarcely charitable in his dealings with them.[2] But above all, he has been criticised on grounds of alleged fickleness, for his sometimes rapid and often drastic changes of mind, his transfers of allegiance from one party or politician to another. The pattern for these attacks was set by 'Orion' (Jean Maze) in his *Nouveau dictionnaire des girouettes*, inspired by Alexis Eymeri's original dictionary of turncoats of 1815. Mauriac's refusal to read the book and Maze's subsequent reply assured publicity for the latter's method, which consisted simply of juxtaposing conflicting declarations by Mauriac, and which came to be adopted by Jean Nocher and Maurice Schumann.[3] Mauriac often denied his inconsistency, arguing that his shifts of opinion were always due to changed circumstances and conditioned by the need to serve the truth as he saw it at any given moment: constancy in pursuit of truth was more important than habit at the ballot-box.[4] His defence is a convincing one, and it is doubtful in any case whether many politicians or political writers would emerge better than Mauriac does from a close study of changing views and contradictory statements.

Most of the comments on Mauriac's work as a journalist have been motivated by the desire to discredit him. No critic has yet combined objectivity with an examination of the structure of his polemical attitudes. And yet it is here, in the underlying suppositions and, it is tempting to say, myths of Mauriac's politics that the interest and at the same time the weaknesses of his position lie.

When faced with a political idea, there were basically only two questions that Mauriac asked himself. The first was: are the spiritual and moral assumptions from which it takes root such that I, as a Christian, can give it my support without offending my conscience or bringing into disrepute or ridicule the faith of which I am a public representative? And the second: what will be the consequences, in terms of my country's prestige at home and abroad, if this idea is translated into political action? Here lie the dual foundations of Mauriac's politics: in his Christianity and in his patriotism.

He stressed time and again that in politics his guiding light was his Christian moral code. 'Je n'ai point (. . .) à défendre mes positions politiques,' he writes, 'elles sont étroitement liées à ma foi religieuse.'[5] Not only did he identify politics and morality; he also decried any attempt to dissociate the two. The separation of the two planes was the real crime, in his eyes, of Nazi Germany.[6] It was this division that had bathed the world in blood.[7] And even in peace-time the spiritual struggle is inseparable from the political one. Every political battle is part of a war of religion.[8]

The undesirable separation of the political from the moral law usually manifested itself, for Mauriac, in the conception of human nature reflected in any given political creed. The war was 'un débat où il y allait de la conception même que nous nous faisons de la créature humaine et de son destin terrestre'.[9] He even tried to base on this conviction a theory of the political spectrum. What were the essential differences between the Left and Right in politics? Did they not resolve themselves into, on the one hand, faith in Man, and on the other, mistrust and scorn of human nature leading to a belief that Man is unworthy of justice and liberty?[10] The left-winger stood in the lineage of Rousseau, with his legendary optimism towards Man's innate goodness. The extreme form of this view was no doubt naïve, for fervent Rousseauists were over-indulgent in their view of human nature, forgetting that it was tainted by the Fall.[11] But such naïvety is preferable to the cynicism of the opposing belief, on which was based the ideology of Nazi Germany—those doctrines of death that denied the Redemption.[12] Those who scorn Man are in open revolt against

Christ, and they are to be found, in Mauriac's system, on the Right. This belief is one of the constants of his politics and helps to explain his continual stigmatization of the Right from the time of the Spanish Civil War onwards, and his attacks on Mollet and the Socialists or on the M.R.P. when he deemed their policies to have swung to the Right. Yet it leads him into all manner of difficulties. According to his theory, the man of the Left believes in justice and human perfectibility. There is clearly no allowance here for the possibility of tyranny within a socialist system, no place for Stalin. Mauriac's reversal of attitudes towards the Communists in the post-war years reflects this embarrassment. In the Cold War, he wrote, two ethical systems were locked in battle, each with a view of Man and History that was irreconcilable with that of the adversary.[13] Yet to fit the logic of his theory, given that one of these groups was the humanist and 'Christian' West, Stalinist Russia would have to be categorised as a right-wing state. This, on Mauriac's purely moral plane, where 'Right' equals 'totalitarian', would be an arguable view, and a polemically potent one in the France of the late 1940s. Yet it obviously begs the question of where the economic structure of societies comes in. The dividing line, as far as economic outlook is concerned, between the French Socialists —who, of course, are Marxists—and Communists, whether in France or in Russia, is one that Mauriac never plots. Instead, he saw the Socialists merely as humanists. Their sharing of power with the M.R.P. in the post-war Tripartite coalition (the Communists being the third party involved) brought together 'le courant humaniste et le courant chrétien'.[14] Thus Mauriac's distinction between Right and Left not only begins as a moral one. It never develops, never reaches out from the moral sphere to apply itself to political and economic factors. What takes place is not so much a merging of the two realms as a confusion of them. Thus Mauriac could write, in 1957, that all those who protested against the government's Algerian policy were Christians even if they did not know it,[15] thereby claiming knowledge, apparently, of the unconscious religious conversion of M. Jean-Paul Sartre.

His changing attitude to the M.R.P. is one of the most illuminating examples of the effect of this confusion of issues. Although expecting the party to implement a policy based on the Christian values to which its members held as individuals, he had no practical advice to offer on the application of such values to everyday politics, and showed no understanding of the various economic, military and political pressures which can prevent any party in power from realising its ideals, and which, numerous in any governmental system, were multiplied in the uneasy coalition governments in which the M.R.P. found itself sharing. Yet he chose to castigate the party for its 'non-Christian' and its 'right-wing' policies. What in practical terms would constitute a Christian policy was a question Mauriac did not try to answer. When the Christian democrat Étienne Borne asked what would be the political lesson to be drawn from the Sermon on the Mount, he replied that it would be recognised by its results: fewer political crimes, less bloodshed, greater love of France in the Third World.[16]

He was imprecise also in associating the cause of the Western world with that of Christianity. World peace, he said, depended on the outcome of the debate between Christian spirituality and Marxist materialism,[17] the combat of the two Cities—that of the Spirit and that of deified Matter.[18] But he did not define in what ways the aims of the West are those of the Spirit, or how they are less materialistic than the ideology (even supposing such a monolithic entity exists) of the Eastern bloc. He proceeded by a simple system of negatives and positives. Soviet ideology rejects the Gospels (he once summarised the career of Krushchev as a forty-year combat against God)[19]; therefore the Western adversaries of Russia accept them. But, not surprisingly, he detected few real examples of Christian idealism even in the West. What he saw instead were the machinations of a sinister figure to whom he gave the symbolic name of Machiavelli. This was the pragmatist, the unscrupulous opportunist who defied Christian morality. Machiavelli, he said, was the father of the mass crime, its organiser and theoretical justifier.[20] The world was full of modern Machiavellis, and the role of Christians was to oppose them.[21] The Christian's historic battle with evil was a conflict with History itself. 'L'Histoire'—a word to which Mauriac, like de Gaulle, invariably gives a capital letter, as if it were some personified force—is for him permeated with evil.[22] 'Elle se fait', he says, 'elle se tisse jour après jour, nous y sommes tous engagés; elle nous presse de toutes parts et même dans la mort, nous ne saurions nous en évader.[23] The mysterious destination to which History drags the human race may well have been revealed in 1945, at Hiroshima and Nagasaki. 'La désagrégation de la matière, he warned, 'c'était donc vers cet anéantissement que les peuples marchaient; c'était vers le suicide planétaire.[24] And in this march towards the final eclipse of humanity, History is guilty of murder every day, the murder of Love:

> Quelqu'un m'a dit un jour, et je ne l'ai jamais oublié: 'C'est
> l'amour que nous avons crucifié, et que nous continuons de
> crucifier jusqu'à la fin du monde.' C'est cela l'Histoire, et il n'y a
> pas d'autre Histoire.[25]

This accumulated series of murders, of crucifixions, led him to define
History further as the sum total of individual sins:

> Je la considère comme la somme, comme le total effroyable
> de nos convoitises, depuis le meurtre d'Abel. *Libido sciendi, libido
> sentiendi, libido dominandi*, ces trois fleuves de feu alimentent cette
> Histoire qui roule et précipite des civilisations, l'une après
> l'autre, dans le même néant.[26]

This, to him, was the key to the meaning of war:

> Les guerres, bien loin d'être l'œuvre de Dieu, (sont) au
> contraire le total de tous les crimes les plus cachés, l'égoût
> collecteur de toutes les souillures, ce qu'il y a de moins divin en
> ce monde et de plus humain, voilà ce que je crois.[27]

As this last passage shows History is not, as might at first be supposed, a malevolent force external to Man, but a power within him,
and which bears the mark of his dual nature. Regimes rise and fall,
Mauriac wrote, all of them good and bad at the same time because they
partake of Man's division. History is both hero and criminal, created
in Man's image.[28] But Man is also free, and therefore if there is more
crime than heroism in History, this the fault of those concerned in its
making. Who had permitted the forces of darkness to engulf the
world, Mauriac asked in 1939, but Man himself?[29] Likewise, the
drama of Morocco and the catastrophe of Indochina were not born
of a fatality, not preordained from all time; they could have been
avoided.[30] Mauriac did not believe in the fatality of History: 'Le
vouloir d'un petit nombre d'hommes la détermine.'[31] He could see no
evidence, in the midst of this Man-made political error and evil, of a
direct intervention on the part of God. He had expressed the hope that
God might intervene in Spain,[32] but in 1949 he felt obliged to admit to
Camus:

> Si vous me poussez sur ce terrain et me demandez quelle
> place je laisse à la Providence dans l'Histoire, je vous répondrai
> que notre Dieu est le Dieu des cœurs. Je connais, je puis le dire,
> je touche, j'adore sa présence dans les cœurs. Qu'il soit béni pour
> cette grâce dont j'ai tant abusé. Mais l'Histoire, ce sont les
> hommes, les passions des hommes, qui l'écrivent.[33]

At times he even wondered if God had not abandoned, in anguish, his warring creatures. The silence of God in the world of politics was as terrifying in our age, he wrote, as it had been to Victor Hugo when, in 1837, he had written:

> Dans tout ce grand éclat d'un siècle éblouissant,
> Une chose, ô Jésus, en secret m'épouvante,
> C'est l'écho de ta voix qui va s'affaiblissant.[34]

Yet in more optimistic moments Mauriac declared that Grace was active in the world, combating the Nature—collective human nature —that was History. Modern Man had deified History, but the Incarnation too was part of that History[35]. The evil men who were so often History's agents served to remind others of the inhumanity which only a miracle can counter; such was the role, in the perspective of eternity, of Hitler. But the miracle needed to combat him and other evil men takes place every day, through Christ's presence in men's souls.[36]

For Grace, although it did not take the form of a direct intervention, could be seen at work in the actions of certain great men, or more precisely, one great man. Mauriac heralded the return to power of de Gaulle as follows: 'Je crois que sa présence à cet instant de notre Histoire est un signe: le signe que nous ne sommes pas abandonnés, malgré tant de fautes.'[37] De Gaulle, often called the Man of Destiny, was to Mauriac the Man of Grace.[38] His political contentment during most of de Gaulle's reign ('ce temps de grâce')[39] depended partly on an interpretation of the role of this period in History which has less to do with political science than with Mauriac's own peculiar theology. The drama of grace, free will, divine intervention or remoteness, which is the basis of the structure of his fictional world, provides him also with a framework for his political outlook. The secular, godless force of History is the product of a humanity tainted from the start by the sin of Adam. 'C'est par le biais de l'Histoire', he wrote, 'que j'arrive à entrer un peu dans le mystère du péché originel: ce mystère de la solidarité des fils d'Eve dans le mal.'[40] It is an endless succession of political crimes perpetrated by men who have abused the free will accorded them by God and who live in isolation from Him, by their rejection of Him or His abandonment of them. This is the drama, varying in degrees of atrocity, of Hitler, Mussolini and Stalin, who consciously opted for Evil over Good; the drama also of Franco, of Maurras, who tried to harness Good to the ultimate career of Evil; and of the men of the Fourth Republic whose inability to halt the inexorable progression towards destruction reached criminal proportions. The sole ray of hope in this renegade political universe emanated from the one-man elect called Charles de Gaulle, unique among statesmen by the grace bestowed upon him by God and which gives him the will and the strength to suspend the headlong rush to national evil. For de Gaulle's achievements are finally identified by Mauriac as being in accordance with what Christians as well as humanists should wish:

> De Gaulle s'est dressé (. . .) pour inscrire dans les faits, au nom de l'État restauré, cette politique à la fois humaine et chrétienne que nous avions, nous, dans l'esprit et dans le cœur, et que nous avons été impuissants à incarner.[41]

Not many observers of the political scene, and probably not even de Gaulle himself, would describe the Gaullist mission in such terms. Mauriac's picture, at this point, is clearly a long way from reality. His insistence on viewing politics from the point of view of religious belief has led him astray. 'Moi qui chemine seul,' he once said, 'j'ai la certitude d'appartenir au petit nombre de ceux qui tiennent une lampe au cœur des ténèbres.'[42] His light, however, was pointed only in the direction dictated by his preoccupations as a Catholic novelist, and if it illuminates at all, it does so only partially and at one level. There are crucial areas of politics of which Mauriac had no understanding, and in which he showed little interest—notably the whole field of economics. Even Barrès would have told him that economics is the central factor in politics[43] and that myth-making can only be a stimulant, not a basis for true understanding.[44] De Gaulle, too, by reputation no economist either, yet possessed the awareness of the gulf between myth and reality: myths, he once complained, were a hindrance once one was expected to live up to them.[45] That Barrès and de Gaulle were professional politicians while Mauriac was not explains a great deal about their truer grasp on political reality.

This is not to argue that Mauriac's place as a journalist was a superfluous one. There is always room in political journalism for the voice of moral conscience and for a watchdog over the activities of politicians. Mauriac's presence ensured that someone was there to stand for justice and humanity, and this was a role he filled to great effect, and with considerable moral and physical courage, in his protest against the slaughter in Spain, supposedly carried out for the Christian cause; in his participation in the Resistance; in his stand during the *épuration*; in his attacks on the politicians of the Fourth Republic, especially over such issues as the use of torture in Algeria. Even his support of de Gaulle during the terrorist campaign of the O.A.S. can only add to this honourable list. It was all the harder for him to take such positions, especially those of the period 1936–1944, in that he was in a minority amongst Catholics. His contribution to the severance of Catholicism from extreme, reactionary politics was undoubtedly an important one. His was not the pioneering role in this, but his adhesion, as a prestigious writer and establishment figure, to the cause of liberal Catholicism for which other, less well-known men were fighting in the 1930s gave that movement much needed weight.

The central importance, in Mauriac's contribution to the liberalisation of Catholic politics, of his relationship to Maurras and the Action Française has been amply illustrated, and it is to this relationship that we must once more turn in order to define the second crucial strand in his outlook, his patriotism. Towards the end of his life, Mauriac expressed a debt to Maurras which it had not been possible for him to admit so overtly in earlier days when the epithet 'Maurrassian' carried such a stigma. Maurras had taught him that the party system, such as it operated in France, was taking the nation to its death as a great power. In this lesson, Mauriac confessed, lay the seeds of his admiration for the Fifth Republican constitution and for the man who had created it in order to rescue the nation from the stagnation of inter-party warfare.[46] He had been willing, during the first few years of the Fourth Republic, to give parliamentary democracy a chance to work; it had seemed at the time the only possible system in the wake of the totalitarian dictatorships. But the instability of the Fourth Republic had proved Maurras right on this point, just as it had proved right de Gaulle, himself a sympathetic reader of Maurrassian anti-parliamentary polemic. Did Mauriac's support for de Gaulle, whom he described to Claude Mauriac in 1944 as a man in the Maurrassian mould, mean that his retrospective view of Maurrassian nationalism had changed after 1958? The answer is that it had not. He had always accepted, at heart, the view that France needed a powerful leader, his actions untrammelled by the objections of lesser men. That this was also Maurras' view did not make an absolute Maurrassian of Mauriac any more than it did of de Gaulle. This one area of agreement apart, it was in their common divergences of outlook from that of Maurras that Mauriac and de Gaulle most significantly concurred. To understand this is to begin to understand Mauriac's importance and that of de Gaulle as exemplars, on the theoretical level, of a new post-Maurrassian nationalism.

Mauriac's religious differences with Maurras have been described, and need no reiteration. They perhaps seemed less important to Mauriac, in his decline, than they had before. At least, he conceded, Maurras was sincere about his agnosticism; he was much less reprehensible than Franco, who had insisted on the Christian nature of his anti-Republican crusade.[47] The real, profound difference between Mauriac and Maurras, on the plane of nationalist ideology, lay elsewhere.

The chief characteristic of Maurras' system is its exclusiveness, both ethnic and historical. Jews and *métèques* were not truly French, did not possess a genetic predisposition to be moved by an appeal to collective French-ness. Un-French also, in the sense of running counter to what was most noble in national tradition, was the whole trend of French history since the Revolution. Maurras' quarrel with the Republicans resolved itself into a conflict between opposing concepts of the French nation. To him and the vast number of Action Française followers, France had only been truly France under the *Ancien Régime*. To a hard-line Republican, equally exclusive in this respect, France's long pre-revolutionary history had been a false trail; since 1789 the nation had groped her way towards the right path and had hit upon it after 1870.

Mauriac's outlook was different. Not only did he oppose racialism in all its forms—as he illustrated by his many personal friendships, at the time of the crises in North Africa, with members of that Arab race which, since the war, has replaced the Jewish one as the focal point of French racialism; but he also eschewed the kind of selective historiography that divided Royalist from Republican. France had had her heroes and villains on both sides of the Revolution. Mauriac, notoriously more interested in sinners than saints, was especially good at picking out the villains:

> Notre histoire me fascine et m'horrifie. Si je ne craignais de faire rire, j'avouerais qu'une part de moi-même ne s'est jamais consolée de la croisade albigeoise, jamais consolée de la Saint-Barthélémy, ni des dragonnades, ni de la destruction de Port-Royal, ni de la Terreur, ni du procès de la Reine, ni du marytre de Louis XVII, ni de tout le reste, jusqu'à la dernière torture, en Algérie, du dernier torturé.[48]

And when, in 1968, his anguished defence of Gaullist order led him to echo Jacques Bainville's view of the Monarchy as the 'fil conducteur' on which the cohesion of the nation had originally depended,[49] this was not a plea for a literal return to a hereditary system, but an argument in favour of authoritarian republicanism of the Fifth Republican type, which, as a kind of modern monarchy, incorporated the best of pre- and post-revolutionary traditions.

On both levels, ethnic and historical, Mauriac was a national integrationist rather than an integral nationalist. That he could plausibly say the same of de Gaulle was the key to the firm ideological bond between them. De Gaulle's acceptance of all Frenchmen, whatever their ethnic origins, and his recognition of the totality of French history (with the exceptions of Vichy and the Fourth Republic) may have contained a greater element of calculation than Mauriac's more instinctively tolerant attitude; but they were important components of the 'certaine idée'. The Parisian townscape which he paints in the epic opening sequence of his war memoirs is highlighted by symbols of glory that are consciously chosen from a variety of epochs and institutions in the nation's past: Notre-Dame (medieval and Catholic), Versailles (monarchical and classical), the Arc de Triomphe and the Invalides (Napoleonic, imperial, revolutionary and military).[50] And an incidental comment in Le Salut on the alliance of European nations against revolutionary France in the 1790s is illuminating: Maurras would never have written 'la France', as de Gaulle does, to describe the target of the monarchies, but 'la Révolution'[51]. At a deep intellectual level, de Gaulle, like Mauriac, had sloughed off the Maurrassian narrowness to which he was potentially as prone as most patriots. Though he fully shared Maurras' and Bainville's belief in force as an agent of civilising change, he had married this concept, probably deliberately, to the revolutionary and republican one of progress as early as Le Fil de l'épée: 'Il faut cette accoucheuse (la Force) pour tirer au jour le progrès,' he had written; '(. . .) On lui doit (à la Force) tour à tour l'ordre et la liberté'.[52] The order of the authoritarian, the liberty of the revolutionary: both, in certain circumstances, could be the end which justified forcible means. (De Gaulle himself, of course, had been a revolutionary, on the plane of legality if not on the more elevated one of legitimacy, at the time of Vichy.) Also, while agreeing with Maurras that a great national leader must be found—for Man, he said, needs to be governed as much as he needs to be fed—he did not restrict the choice of that leader by the imposition of a hierarchical system like Maurras', but welcomed the rise of any individual with the vision and energy to lead his nation.[53] Certainly anti-egalitarian, de Gaulle was no anti-individualist. He was the man at whose feet Mauriac would have fallen in 1918 when instead he mistakenly looked to Maurras for a combination of these attitudes.[54] Unlike Maurras also, de Gaulle had no instinctive fear of change, not even in old age, and no absolute belief in traditions—indeed, he preferred to use the less emotionally charged term 'conventions',[55] which suggested a willingness to revise institutions (French Algeria, for instance) when the time came. And if, like Maurras, he had a deep respect for pragmatism, and rational judgment in the face of military and political problems, he stressed also, taking Bergson as his model, the value of instinct and inspiration[56]—terms which Maurras would have labelled 'romantic' and, given their attributed source, 'Jewish'.

It is in describing de Gaulle's width of historical and intellectual tolerance that Mauriac most clearly reveals his own and, at the same time, marks their common difference from Maurras:

> Maurras, (. . .) lui, éliminait ce qu'il haïssait et menait sa guerre civile personnelle à travers l'histoire. De Gaulle, il me semble, ne choisit pas: Robespierre et Saint-Just entrent dans la composition du tableau au même titre que Saint-Louis et que Jeanne d'Arc.[57]

But lest it be thought that Mauriac was simply following in de Gaulle's footsteps in this respect, it is necessary to point out that he himself had quoted with respect the words of men of the Revolution, especially Saint-Just, during the Occupation, when de Gaulle was as yet a remote figure across the Channel. And in the immediate postwar period, when he was not yet fully under the spell of the General, he had shown the same eclecticism in his bid to reconcile warring factions: 'La vie spirituelle de la France est trop ancienne et trop riche pour ne pas avoir suscité plusieurs espèces de familles.'[58]

Patriots, and sharing with nationalist historians like Bainville and Gaxotte a certain conception of history as a succession of great deeds done by great men (no room here for the niceties of social and economic history), Mauriac and de Gaulle were nevertheless not Maurrassians. They had more in common, ideologically, with that other giant of French nationalism, Barrès, in whose writings they could have found (and where Mauriac, probably, did find) a foreshadowing of many of their own beliefs. Barrès, anti-parliamentarian, campaigner for personal rule by a charismatic leader, was nonetheless a greater realist than Maurras: he accepted the Republic as a fact, and a permanent one. Yet he argued that men could rally to the nation just as passionately and effectively if it were governed by a strong Republican president as they would when moved by loyalty to a hereditary monarch: it is the national idea itself that promotes the willing absorption of the individual within the community. De Gaulle believed this too. His account of his triumphant march, on the afternoon of Saturday, August 26th, 1944, from the Étoile to Notre-Dame, confirms it. Of the two million people who cheered him on his way from the symbolic heart of French military greatness to the symbolic temple of her spirituality, he writes: 'Dans cette communauté, qui n'est qu'une seule pensée, un seul élan, un seul cri, les différences s'effacent, les individus disparaissent.'[59] The whole passage, recounting 'un de ces miracles de la conscience nationale',[60] is a glorious set-piece of nationalist literature. It recalls unmistakably the account, in Les Déracinés, of another national occasion, another ritual procession attended by Frenchmen who unite around an embodiment of Frenchness: the funeral of Victor Hugo, the carriage of his body from the Pantheon to the Arc de Triomphe for the spiritual union of Poet and Emperor.[61] Unity is a keynote in Barrèsian nationalism as it is in that of de Gaulle and Mauriac. Despite his anti-Dreyfusism, Barrès later accepted the Jews as one of France's spiritual peoples, to be integrated, not spurned. His nationalism, as Jean-Marie Domenach argues, is more open and attractive than that of the Maurrassian mainstream, and it leads directly to the nationalism of de Gaulle:

> Le nationalisme français, s'il fût demeuré plus fidèle à Barrès, n'aurait pas subi les suites de ce refus opposé par les maurrassiens à toute une part de la tradition française, de cette aigreur vaine qui se condamne à déchirer ce qu'elle prétend sauver; il aurait gardé ce style intégrateur, ample et noble, cet esprit de rassemblement qu'imposera, après la défaite de 1940, l'homme qui devait être, bien autrement que Boulanger, le général barrésien.[62]

There was, however, one obvious circumstantial difference between Barrès and de Gaulle that prevented the permanent transposition of this ideological similarity to the plane of political reality. Barrès, as far as power was concerned, was doomed to cry impotently in the wilderness, whereas in his nationalist descendant de Gaulle the national idea came to power, to supreme power. This power did not necessarily corrupt de Gaulle, for he remained rigidly faithful to the end to his own concept of personal honour, but it did damage his claim to be a consistent unifier of his people. In his final intolerance of the opponents of his own brand of legitimacy, de Gaulle's regime was in the end, as 1968 suggested, a divisive one. In that Mauriac shared and even surpassed the General's intransigence, his reputation as an integrator was compromised too. Paradoxically, a close reading of

Barrès' views on the role of regional autonomy in the encouragement of love for the entire nation[63] might have forewarned either man of one of the strongest objections to the centralised bureaucracy of the Fifth Republic.

Between Barrès and Mauriac too, there were both similarities and differences. Mauriac almost certainly took from Barrès the arguments he used to defend de Gaulle against charges of Caesarism and dictatorship. The difference between Bonaparte and Boulanger, in Barrès' view, and between Bonaparte and de Gaulle in Mauriac's was identical: it lay in the elimination of precisely that hereditary element, that dynasty-building, which was to Maurras the cement of French institutional stability.[64] Likewise, each man argued in very similar terms that his support of personal rule was not undemocratic. 'Je suis un démocrate', Barrès makes his Boulanger say, 'et non pas un partisan de ce corps parlementaire où chacun pense à ses intérêts, jamais à ceux de la patrie.'[65] And Mauriac echoes: 'En quoi cette forme de démocratie'— the Gaullist plebiscitary variety, by-passing the quarrelsome parties— 'est-elle moins démocratique, si j'ose dire, que celle qui s'exprimait dans la Constitution de 1875?'[66]

It is interesting to note how often the name of Barrès recurs in Mauriac's articles of the middle and late 1960s. The earliest intellectual influence on him had also proved the most durable, although not in the way the rebellious young reader of the apparently iconoclastic *Culte du moi* had imagined. But still there was the great gulf between them carved out by faith on the one hand and religious scepticism on the other, and for Mauriac a corresponding gulf between nationalism and Christianity which Barrès, as an agnostic, did not have to cross. Here lies the final question which must be asked about Mauriac's politics. That he was a leading Christian observer of his age is accepted; that he was also an important nationalist writer has emerged from this present study. But were there two Mauriacs or one? Did he succeed in reconciling his Christianity with his nationalism? For in the end national prestige resolves itself into a question of power, as Maurras and de Gaulle recognised. It is even harder for nations than it is for individuals to turn the other cheek. Politics, as Barrès also taught, is an amoral world. 'On ne leur reproche pas leur bassesse ni leur cynisme', Barrès comments on his political intriguers in *Les Déracinés*, 'c'est par des personnages bas et des moyens cyniques que de très grandes choses ont été accomplies.'[67] Less hard-bitten nationalist writers have often been embarrassed by the amorality of their heroes.

In a desperate attempt to explain Saint-Louis' summary executions of the barons who opposed him, Bainville writes: 'Il y a aussi une sainteté de l'ordre et des institutions.'[68] But Bainville was playing with words.

Mauriac's attempts to reconcile the two strands in his outlook are no more convincing. France, since Pépin le Bref came to the aid of the Papacy against the Lombards, has been able to claim the title of Eldest Daughter of the Church, and thus respect for national tradition could be seen as reverence for an instinctively Christian nation; but this was a specious argument, and Mauriac knew it. His identification of left-wing humanist tradition with Christian values, his frequent references to the mission of post-revolutionary France as a moral teacher of liberty to the world, are equally vague. His commendation of de Gaulle as a man who ultimately worked for causes that all Christians can support borders on the ludicrous. Worse, Mauriac's gleeful admiration of French stability and efficiency which, ignoring the Fourth Republic's role in creating its foundations, he attributed to de Gaulle, ended by eroding his own moral consistency. One of the characteristics of de Gaulle which he admired most was the man's pragmatism; and some of this pragmatism attached itself in due course to the Christian moralist who had poured so much energy into denunciations of Maurrassian 'realism'. Mauriac came close to emulating his political arch-demons in separating the moral from the political. 'A quoi sert en politique,' he once asked, 'd'avoir raison et d'être toujours battu? La foi chrétienne suffit à soutenir mon exigence d'absolu. Je suis politiquement pragmatiste.'[69] These words, written as early as 1958, were something of a *boutade*. But in the closing years of his life, the truth they contained was clearly revealed. Mauriac was scarcely inspired by Christian sentiments in his acrimonious onslaughts on the Anglo-Saxons, on those who were Europeans first and Frenchmen second, on the young people who resented the imposition upon them of an old man's 'certaine idée de la France'. Just as his Christianity prevented him from being a Maurrassian nationalist, so did Mauriac's Gaullist nationalism stand in the way of his consistent observation of world affairs from a pure Christian viewpoint. Had he died twelve years earlier, or had de Gaulle never returned to power, Mauriac would probably not have established his claims to be regarded as a major nationalist writer. But he would have finished his days as a respected Christian commentator on the foibles of men and nations. Posterity will have to decide which of the two mutually exclusive epitaphs is the nobler.

SELECTIVE BIBLIOGRAPHY

(The place of publication is, for French books, Paris and for books in English, London, unless otherwise indicated.)

1. Mauriac's principal writings on politics:

Le Bâillon dénoué, Grasset, 1945. (OC XI.)
Le Bloc-notes, 5 vols., Flammarion, 1958–71.
Le Cahier noir, Editions de Minuit, 1943 (published under the pseudonym 'Forez'). (OC XI.)
De Gaulle, Grasset, 1964.
Journal, especially vols. 4 and 5, Flammarion,1950 and 1953. The first three volumes (Grasset 1934–40) also contain some political material. (OC XI.)
Journal d'un homme de trente ans, Egloff, 1948. (OC IV.)
Journal du temps de l'occupation. (OC XI.)
Mémoires politiques, Grasset, 1967 (some of the articles in this collection also appear in the volumes listed above).
La Nation française a une âme, Comité national des écrivains, 1943. (OC XI.)

Prefaces to:

R. Barrat, *Justice pour le Maroc*, Seuil, 1953.
A. Dreyfus, *Cinq années de ma vie*, Fasquelle, 1962.
B. Just, *Un procès préfabriqué*, Éditions du 'Témoignage chrétien', 1949.
'A. Sidobré' (pseudonym of Maurice Schumann), *Le Germanisme en marche*, Éditions du Cerf, 1938.
V. Montserrat, *Le Drame d'un peuple inconnu: la guerre au pays basque*, Peyre, 1938.

Reference is also made in this book to articles by Mauriac, not collected in the above volumes, which appeared in the following newspapers or periodicals: *Le Figaro*, *La Revue fraternelle* (Bordeaux), *La Revue hebdomadaire*, *La Revue Montalembert*, *La Revue du Temps présent*.

A considerable number of other works by Mauriac have also been mentioned. Full details are given in the references, and it would serve little purpose to include a lengthy list here. A list of all of Mauriac's books and most of his articles (up to 1960) is provided in the indispensable *Essai de bibliographie chronologique* of Keith Goesch (Nizet, 1965).

2. Other primary sources quoted:

Bainville, *Histoire de France*, Fayard, 1924.
Barrès, *Le Culte du moi, Les Déracinés, L'Appel au soldat*, in *L'Œuvre de Maurice Barrès*,

Au Club de l'Honnête homme, vols. 1–4, 1965; and *Le Bi-centenaire de Jean-Jacques Rousseau*, Éditions de l'Indépendance, 1912.

Barrès/Maurras, correspondence: *La République ou le roi*, Plon, 1970.

De Gaulle: *Mémoires de guerre*, 3 vols., Livre de poche, 1954–9; *Mémoires d'espoir*, vol. 1, Livre de poche, 1970; *Le Fil de l'épée*, 10/18, 1962.

Gide, *Retour de l'U.R.S.S.*, Gallimard, 1950.

Maurras, *Œuvres capitales*, vol. 2, Flammarion, 1954; *L'Ordre et le désordre*, Éditions Self, 1948.

3. Books and articles on Mauriac's politics, or which contain substantial sections on the subject:

M. Bardèche, *Lettre à François Mauriac*, La Pensée libre, 1947.

R.-L. Bruckberger, *Nous n'irons plus au bois*, Amiot-Dumont, 1948.

J. Debû-Bridel, *La Résistance intellectuelle*, Julliard, 1970.

J. de Fabrègues, *Mauriac*, Plon, 1971.

J. E. Flower, 'François Mauriac and Social Catholicism', *French Studies*, April 1967; *Intention and Achievement*, Oxford, Clarendon Press, 1969.

X. Grall, *Mauriac journaliste*, Éditions du Cerf, 1960.

L. Guitard, *Lettre sans malice à François Mauriac sur la mort du général Weygand et quelques autres sujets*, Martineau, 1967.

J. Laurent, *Mauriac sous de Gaulle*, La Table ronde, 1964.

C. Mauriac, *Un autre de Gaulle*, Hachette, 1970.

J. Maze, 'François Mauriac inventeur', *Écrits de Paris*, June 1950; and, under the pseudonym 'Orion', *Nouveau dictionnaire des girouettes*, Éditions le Régent, 1948.

J. Nocher, *Pamphlet atomique, n° 18: Sadiques contemporains*, Davy, 1949.

R. Rémond, *Les Catholiques, le communisme et les crises, 1929–1939*, Colin, 1960.

M. Scott, 'The Sillon and Mauriac's first published writings', *Forum for Modern Language Studies*, April 1971.

M. Schumann, *Le Vrai malaise des intellectuels de gauche*, Plon, 1957.

R. Speaight, *François Mauriac: a study of the man and the writer*, Chatto & Windus, 1976.

P. Vandromme, *La Politique littéraire de François Mauriac*, Etheel, 1957.

Cahiers François Mauriac (Vol. 4, Grasset, 1976) contains the following articles relevant to the subject of this present book: G.-P. Collet, 'François Mauriac et le Sillon'; P. Croc, 'François Mauriac et Maurice Barrès'; J. Touzot, 'Mauriac et les grands écrivains journalistes'.

François Mauriac (collection Génies et Réalités, Hachette, 1977) contains articles by J. Daniel on 'François Mauriac et le journalisme' and by J.-M. Domenach on 'L'Itinéraire politique de François Mauriac'.

4. Other works. I am especially indebted to the following:

J. Duquesne, *Les Catholiques français sous l'occupation*, Grasset, 1966.

J. de Fabrègues, *Le Sillon de Marc Sangnier*, Perrin, 1964.

E. Weber, *Action Française*, Stanford University Press, 1962.

There is neither space nor necessity to list all of the many books I have consulted in search of information on the history and political thought of the period. The following are quoted or referred to in my text:

R. Aron, *Histoire de l'épuration*, vol. 2, Fayard, 1959.

I.-P. Barko, *L'Esthétique littéraire de Charles Maurras*, Droz, Geneva, 1961.

L. Bodin & J. Touchard, *Front populaire, 1936*, Colin, 1961.

B. Crozier, *De Gaulle*, 2 vols., Eyre-Methuen, 1973.

A. Dansette, *Histoire religieuse de la France contemporaine sous la 3ème République*, Flammarion, 1951.

J. de Fabrègues, *Charles Maurras et son Action Française*, Perrin, 1966.

Mgr. Harscouet, *Modernisme social*, Editions du Cèdre, 1952.

A. Hartley, *Gaullism*, Routledge & Kegan Paul, 1972.

R. Havard de la Montagne, *Histoire de l'Action Française*, Amiot-Dumont, 1950.

P. Lasserre, *Le Romantisme français*, Garnier, 1919.

C. Mauriac, *Conversations avec André Gide*, Albin Michel, 1951.

J. Mauriac, *Mort du général de Gaulle*, Grasset, 1972.

P. A. Ouston, *The Imagination of Maurice Barrès*, University of Toronto Press, 1974.

R. Paxton, *Vichy France*, Barrie & Jenkins, 1972.

L. Rebatet, *Les Décombres*, Denoël, 1942.

R. Rémond, *La Droite en France*, Aubier, 1954.

H. Thomas, *The Spanish Civil War*, Penguin Books, 1965.

M. Tison-Braun, *La Crise de l'humanisme*, 2 vols., Nizet, 1958, 1967.

A. Werth, *The Strange History of Pierre Mendès-France*, Methuen, 1957.

REFERENCES

Notes and References

When quoting from or referring to articles by Mauriac (other than the *bloc-notes*), I have thought it useful to give in the references their original title, place and date of publication. This is done only on the first occasion on which an article is quoted; on subsequent occasions, I give only the page number of the collected edition in which it can most easily be consulted: it will be easy for the reader to glance back at earlier references and find the complete details if he requires. I have not thought it necessary to provide such information in the case of the *bloc-notes*, which have no title, and the dates of which are given in the collected editions. As far as the place of publication of the *bloc-notes* is concerned, it is sufficient to recall that they appeared regularly in *La Table ronde* from October 1952 to October 1953, in *L'Express* from November 1953 to April 1961 and subsequently in *Le Figaro littéraire*.

The following abbreviations of the most frequently quoted sources are used throughout:

BD: *Le Bâillon dénoué*.

BN I: *Le Bloc-notes, 1952–7*.

BN II: *Le Nouveau Bloc-notes, 1958–60*.

BN III: *Le Nouveau Bloc-notes, 1961–4*.

BN IV: *Le Nouveau Bloc-notes, 1965–7*.

BN V: *Le Dernier Bloc-notes, 1968–70*.

J I: *Journal*, vol. 1.

J IV: *Journal*, vol. 4.

J V: *Journal*, vol. 5.

J 30: *Journal d'un homme de trente ans*.

J Occ: *Journal du temps de l'occupation*.

MP: *Mémoires politiques*.

OC: *Œuvres complètes*, published by Fayard. The Roman numeral following the abbreviation indicates to which of the twelve volumes reference is being made.

PREFACE

1. *Nouveaux mémoires intérieurs*, Flammarion, 1965, p. 243.
2. Vandromme, *La Politique littéraire de François Mauriac*, Etheel, 1957; Laurent, *Mauriac sous de Gaulle*, Table ronde, 1964; Bardèche, *Lettre à François Mauriac*, La Pensée libre, 1947.
3. Éditions du Cerf, 1960.
4. *Mauriac*, Plon, 1971.
5. *François Mauriac: a study of the man and the writer*, Chatto & Windus, 1976.

CHAPTER ONE

1. No full transcript of the lecture has survived, but the anonymous reviewer of the Réunion's regular paper *La Revue Montalembert* gives a clear summary of it, including several lengthy quotations. *La Revue Montalembert*, March 1908.
2. *La Pierre d'achoppement*, Monaco, Éditions du Rocher, 1951, p. 28.
3. BN III, pp. 440-1.
4. *De Gaulle*, Grasset, 1964, p. 85.
5. ibid.
6. MP, p. 13.
7. ibid, p. 30.
8. Quoted in A. Dansette, *Histoire religieuse de la France contemporaine sous la 3 République*, Flammarion, 1951, p. 64.
9. R. Rémond, *La Droite en France*, Aubier, 1954, p. 38.
10. *Les Maisons fugitives*, OC IV, p. 323.
11. *Commencements d'une vie*, OC IV, p. 135.
12. *Ce que je crois*, Grasset, 1962, p. 123.
13. BN IV, p. 306.
14. E. Weber, *Action Française*, Stanford University Press, 1962, p. 35.
15. *Hiver*, OC IV, pp. 344-5.
16. *Mémoires intérieurs*, Flammarion, 1959, p. 125.
17. *La Rencontre avec Barrès*, OC IV, p. 181. Barrès' term *barbare* is capable of meaning all things to all men. Maurras was to borrow it only to use it, in a totally non-Barrèsian sense, to refer to 'nos communards, nos socialistes, nos plèbes' (*La République ou le roi*, Plon, 1970, p. iv). Mauriac's implication that his own *barbares* were the materialistic middle classes of Bordeaux clashes with Barrès' denial that he intends the word to mean 'bourgeois' or 'philistine' (*L'Œuvre de Maurice Barrès*, Au Club de l'Honnête homme, 1965, vol. 1, p. 29). His own more comprehensive definition of a barbarian was 'chacun, hors moi' (*Sous l'œil des barbares*, ibid., p. 107).
18. Especially J. E. Flower, *Intention and Achievement: the novels of François Mauriac*, Oxford, Clarendon Press, 1969, p. 40.
19. *La Rencontre avec Barrès*, OC IV, p. 182.
20. Rémond, op. cit., p. 108.
21. Dansette, op. cit., p. 409.

22. J. de Fabrègues, *Le Sillon de Marc Sangnier*, Perrin, 1964, p. 139. (Henceforth Fabrègues, *Sillon*.)
23. *Modernisme social*, Éditions du Cèdre, 1952.
24. BN V, p. 50.
25. Fabrègues, *Sillon*, p. 181.
26. BN III, p. 386.
27. Fabrègues, *Sillon*, p. 65.
28. *Le Jeune homme*, OC IV, p. 427.
29. BN II, p. 338.
30. cf. M. Scott, 'The Sillon and Mauriac's first published writings' in *Forum for Modern Language Studies*, April 1971.
31. BN II, p. 338.
32. *Nouveaux mémoires intérieurs*, p. 234.
33. MP, p. 14.
34. *Impertinences*, Bloch, 1924, p. 115.
35. J. Folliet in *Témoignage chrétien*, June 9th, 1950.
36. Fabrègues, *Sillon*, pp. 27-9, 40-1, 45-6.
37. Quoted, ibid., p. 26.
38. Quoted, ibid., p. 76.
39. *La Revue fraternelle*, June 1905.
40. ibid., April 1905.
41. *L'Enfant chargé de chaînes*, OC X, p. 8.
42. ibid., p. 27.
43. ibid., p. 24.
44. Flower, op. cit., p. 32.
45. *L'Enfant chargé de chaînes*, OC X, pp. 37 and 33.
46. *Petits essais de psychologie religieuse*, OC VIII, p. 15.
47. ibid., p. 17.
48. ibid., p. 16.
49. *La Rencontre avec Barrès*, OC IV, p. 182.
50. *Amitié de France*, no. 1, February-April 1907.
51. ibid.
52. Fabrègues, *Mauriac*, p. 204.
53. ibid.
54. 'La Jeunesse littéraire' in *La Revue hebdomadaire*, April 1912.
55. *La Maison sur la rive*, Plon, 1914, p. 12.
56. op. cit., p. 519.
57. *Charles Maurras et son Action Française*, Perrin, 1966, p. 257.
58. *La Nation française a une âme*, OC XI, p. 374.
59. The Action Française, true to Maurras' Athenian ideals, was a great encourager of sport. That Mauriac was likely to remain unmoved by its appeal is suggested by a verse portrait of him written by Charles-Francis Caillard, the publisher of his *Les Mains jointes*:
'Le tennis que votre élégance n'aimait pas,
Et le bain que vous ne preniez qu'au bord des vagues.'
(A François Mauriac' in *La Revue du Temps présent*, May 1910.)
60. *Thérèse Desqueyroux*, OC II, p. 183.
61. OC VIII, p. 359.

62. ibid, p. 357.
63. The relationship between *Thérèse Desqueyroux* and Mauriac's view of Rousseau is discussed in fuller form in my article 'Thérèse et Jean-Jacques devant Mauriac', to appear in a special number of *Les Cahiers de l'Herne* in the course of 1980. This article suggests that Mauriac's judgment of Rousseau derives in large measure from his reading of *Trois Réformateurs*, by Jacques Maritain, who was sympathetic, at that time, to the social and moral doctrines of Maurras.
64. BN III, p. 187.
65. *La Rencontre avec Barrès*, OC IV, p. 211.
66. e.g. *Ce que je crois*, p. 15.
67. BN III, p. 172.
68. J. 30, OC IV, p. 232.
69. ibid., p. 225.
70. ibid., p. 232.
71. ibid., pp.231-2.
72. ibid.
73. ibid., p. 248.
74. ibid., p. 255.
75. BN III, p. 412.
76. *Nouveaux mémoires intérieurs*, p. 238.

CHAPTER TWO

1. *Mauriac*, pp. 202-3.
2. M. Chapsal, *Les Écrivains en personne*, Julliard, 1960, p. 136.
3. L. Goldmann, *Pour une sociologie du roman*, Gallimard, 1964, pp. 16, 24.
4. The essay 'L'Homme', first published in *Principes* (1931), can be consulted in *Œuvres capitales*, vol. 2, Flammarian, 1954.
5. *L'Ordre et le désordre*, Éditions Self, 1948, p. 11.
6. *Œuvres capitales*, vol. 2, p. 248.
7. 'La Patrie' in *Mes Idées politiques*; ibid., p. 264.
8. *La Crise de l'humanisme*, vol. 2, Nizet, 1967, p. 194.
9. BN III, p. 138.
10. OC IV, p. 162.
11. *L'Appel au soldat*; *L'Œuvre de Maurice Barrès*, vol. 4, p. 99.
12. *Les Déracinés*; ibid., vol. 3, p. 45.
13. *Bordeaux*, OC IV, pp. 155, 175.
14. *L'Appel au soldat*; *L'Œuvre de Maurice Barrès*, vol. 4, p. 5.
15. *Bordeaux*, OC IV, pp. 155-6.
16. ibid., p. 157.
17. ibid.
18. *Le Jeudi saint*, OC VIII, pp. 174-5.
19. *Un homme libre*; *L'Œuvre de Maurice Barrès*, vol. 1, p. 175.
20. OC VII, preface, p. i.
21. *Illusions perdues*, Garnier, 1956, p. 264.
22. *Œuvres capitales*, vol. 2, pp. 32-3.

23. ibid., p. 34.

24. *L'Ordre et le désordre*, p. 22.

25. *Révolution et romantisme*; *Œuvres capitales*, vol. 2, p. 40.

26. Published in 1907, fifteen years before *Romantisme et révolution*, but written, as Lasserre says in the preface to the 1919 edition, in the lineage of Maurras, whose book of 1922 is merely a definitive statement of views expressed elsewhere for years past.

27. Lasserre, op. cit., Garnier, 1919, p. xvi.

28. I.-P. Barko, *L'Esthétique littéraire de Charles Maurras*, Droz, 1961, p. 133.

29. *Mes grands hommes*, OC VIII, p. 379; *Commencements d'une vie*, OC IV, p. 146; *Mémoires intérieurs*, p. 34, etc.

30. In *Les Mains jointes*.

31. *L'Enfant chargé de chaînes*, OC X, pp. 43-4.

32. ibid., p. 13.

33. Review of Hélène Seguin's *Le Réseau fragile* in *Revue du Temps présent*, January 1910.

34. Review of *Dominique* in *Revue Montalembert*, March 1910.

35. OC VIII, p. 276.

36. OC IV, p. 444.

37. ibid.

38. Dostoyevsky in *Le Roman*, Rimbaud in *Dieu et Mammon*, Proust in *Du côté de chez Proust*, Gide in *Journal d'un homme de trente ans*.

39. BN III, pp. 76, 172, BN IV, p. 257, etc.

40. *La Vie et la mort d'un poète*, OC IV, p. 369.

41. *Romantisme et révolution*, *Œuvres capitales*, vol. 2, pp. 40-1.

42. Introduction to *Le Bienheureux Pie X, sauveur de la France*, *Œuvres capitales*, vol. 2, p. 244.

43. Plon, 1954, p. 21. All references to this edition. (First edition 1929.)

44. *Le Jeune homme*, OC IV, p. 444.

45. OC IV, p. 403.

46. pp. 21-2.

47. *La Rencontre avec Barrès*, OC IV, p. 182.

48. 'Qui triche?' in *L'Écho de Paris*, July 16th, 1932; J I, OC XI, p. 76.

49. *Les Déracinés*; *L'Œuvre de Maurice Barrès*, vol. 3, p. 173.

50. ibid., p. 181.

51. *Le Jeune homme*, OC IV, p. 447.

52. *Thérèse Desqueyroux*, OC II, p. 227.

53. *Souffrances et bonheur du chrétien*, OC VII, p. 240.

54. *Thérèse Desqueyroux*, OC II, p. 170.

55. OC VIII, p. 367.

56. ibid., p. 353.

57. *Thérèse Desqueyroux*, OC II, p. 181.

58. Rousseau, *Religious Writings*, ed. R. Grimsley, Oxford, Clarendon Press, 1970, p. 160.

59. OC VIII, p. 357.

60. *Conscience, instinct divin*, OC II, pp. 510-11.

61. *Thérèse Desqueyroux*, OC II, p. 182.

62. OC VIII, p. 354.

63. ibid., p. 357.

64. *Œuvres capitales*, vol. 2, p. 35.
65. ibid., p. 37.
66. Quoted by P. A. Ouston, *The Imagination of Maurice Barrès*, University of Toronto Press, 1974, p. 5n.
67. *Le Bi-centenaire de Jean-Jacques Rousseau*, Éditions de l'Indépendance, 1912.
68. OC IV, preface, p. ii.
69. *Le Temps*, June 1932.
70. *Le Romancier et ses personnages*, OC VIII, pp. 288-9.
71. *De Bordeaux à Stockholm*, Bordeaux, Delmas, 1953, p. 16.
72. OC IV, preface, p. ii.
73. *Le Mystère Frontenac*, OC IV, p. 123.
74. ibid., p. 86.
75. loc. cit., pp. 18-19.
76. Jarrett-Kerr, *Mauriac*, Cambridge, Bowes & Bowes, 1954, p. 58.
77. Flower, op. cit., pp. 81-94.
78. Bainville, *Histoire de France*, Fayard, 1924, p. 8.
79. cf. *Le Romancier et ses personnages*, OC VIII, p. 290.
80. OC IV, p. 322.
81. J I, OC XI, p. 46.
82. BN IV, p. 47.
83. BN V, p. 214.
84. 'Les Esthètes fascinés', *L'Écho de Paris*, September 10th, 1932, reprinted under title 'Journal de Gide' in J I, OC XI, p. 85.
85. *Retour de l'U.R.S.S.*, Gallimard, 1950, p. 57.
86. *Sept*, July 12th, 1935.
87. J I, OC XI, pp. 50-2.
88. ibid., pp. 79-92.
89. ibid., p. 65. Original article published on July 2nd, 1932.
90. Texts of all relevant articles in R. Rémond, *Les Catholiques, le communisme et les crises 1929–1939*, Colin, 1960, pp. 72-8. Mauriac's article dated January 28th, 1933.
91. Weber, op. cit., p. 579.
92. J I, OC XI, p. 72.
93. *La Pierre d'achoppement*, p. 27.
94. BN V, p. 18.
95. *La Pierre d'achoppement*, p. 27.
96. BN V, p. 19.

CHAPTER THREE

1. 'La Voix de Thorez', *Le Figaro*, April 22nd, 1936; MP, p. 56.
2. 'L'Idée de Nation', *L'Écho de Paris*, July 29th, 1933; MP, p. 39.
3. MP, p. 37.
4. 'Le Scandale et les passions', *L'Écho de Paris*, February 3rd, 1934; MP, p. 471.
5. MP, p. 42.
6. MP, p. 41.
7. 'Le Peuple et les penseurs', *L'Écho de Paris*, April 14th, 1934; MP, pp. 43-6.
8. MP, p. 18.

9. 'Anniversaire du 6 février', *Le Figaro*, February 6th, 1935; MP, pp 47-9.
10. *Esprit*, April 1st, 1935.
11. MP, pp. 56-8.
12. 'La Main tendue', *Le Figaro*, May 26th, 1936; MP, pp. 58-60.
13. 'Un problème humain', *Le Figaro*, March 28th, 1935; MP, pp. 49-51.
14. 'Un dessin de Sennep', *Le Figaro*, September 24th, 1935; MP, pp. 54-5.
15. Chapsal, op. cit., p. 136.
16. 'L'Internationale de la haine', *Le Figaro*, July 25th, 1936. The article has been reprinted in part in L. Bodin & J. Touchard, *Front populaire*, Colin, 1961, p. 174.
17. cf. BN III, pp. 252, 276; BN IV, p. 236.
18. 'A propos des massacres d'Espagne: mise au point', *Le Figaro*, June 30th, 1938; MP, pp. 89-93.
19. 'Badajoz', *Le Figaro*, August 18th, 1936; MP, p. 73.
20. MP, p. 90.
21. ibid., p. 91.
22. Claude Mauriac, *Conversations avec André Gide*, Albin Michel, 1951, p. 107. (Henceforth referred to as Claude Mauriac I).
23. Peyre, 1938, p. 6.
24. Thomas, *The Spanish Civil War*, Penguin Books, 1965, p. 574.
25. 'La Leçon de Shakespeare', *Le Figaro*, February 2nd, 1937; J II, OC XI, p. 200.
26. 'Le Retour du milicien', *Le Figaro*, February 11th, 1937; J II, OC XI, pp. 201-3.
27. Claude Mauriac I, p. 19.
28. *Nouveaux mémoires intérieurs*, pp. 240-1.
29. 'Le Membre souffrant', *Sept*, May 28th, 1937; MP, pp. 81-2.
30. MP, preface, p. 16.
31. *Lettres ouvertes*, Monaco, Éditions du Rocher, 1952, p. 5.
32. Weber, op. cit., p. 384.
33. BN III, p. 350.
34. ibid.
35. ibid., p. 238.
36. ibid., p. 237.
37. ibid., p. 350; MP, p. 18.
38. Weber, op. cit., p. 412.
39. MP, p. 18.
40. *La Rencontre avec Barrès*, OC IV, p. 186.
41. BN III, p. 350.
42. *Nouveaux mémoires intérieurs*, p. 241.
43. 'Le Reste est silence', *Le Temps présent*, June 18th, 1938; MP, p. 102.
44. 'Le Cauchemar dissipé', *Le Temps présent*, October 7th, 1938; MP, p. 108.
45. 'La Grande faim', *Le Temps présent*, October 21st, 1938; MP, p. 109.
46. MP, p. 108.
47. 'Les Intérêts particuliers', *Le Figaro*, March 5th, 1952; MP, p. 292.
48. De Gaulle, *Mémoires de guerre: L'Appel*, Plon., 1954; Livre de Poche edition, p. 31.
49. 'La Vérité', *Le Figaro*, June 19th, 1940; MP, p. 126.
50. Duquesne, *Les Catholiques français sous l'occupation*, Grasset, 1966, p. 26.
51. ibid.

52. ibid., p. 57.
53. 'La France en cellule', *Le Figaro*, July 3rd, 1940; J Occ, OC XI, p. 306.
54. cf. de Gaulle, op. cit., p. 167.
55. R. Paxton, *Vichy France*, Barrie & Jenkins, 1972, p. 46.
56. OC XI, preface, p. ii; MP, preface, p. 20.
57. Vandromme, op. cit., p. 113.
58. MP, p. 125.
59. *Le Pamphlet atomique*, no. 18 (February 1949).
60. BN III, p. 433.
61. BN V, pp. 36-7.
62. 'La Trêve ou la paix', *Le Figaro*, April 1st, 1940; J Occ, OC XI, p. 306.
63. Duquesne, op. cit., p. 165.
64. Denoël, 1942, pp. 49-50.
65. *La Résistance intellectuelle, textes et témoignages réunis et présentés par Jacques Debû-Bridel*, Julliard, 1970, p. 97.
66. Paxton, op. cit., p. 150.
67. Duquesne, op. cit., p. 27.
68. I am indebted to Jacques Duquesne's book (pp. 41-60) for much of this information.
69. Quoted by Weber, op. cit., p. 441.
70. I owe this list to Weber, op. cit.
71. *La Résistance intellectuelle*, p. 59.
72. ibid., p. 100.
73. ibid., p. 60.
74. The text of this declaration is in MP, p. 129.
75. *De Gaulle*, p. 18.
76. De Gaulle, *Mémoires de guerre: L'Appel*, p. 289.
77. De Gaulle, *Mémoires de guerre: L'Unité*, Plon, 1956; Livre de poche edition, p. 174.
78. Crozier, *De Gaulle, I: the Warrior*, Eyre Methuen, 1973, p. 252.
79. ibid.
80. *Le Figaro*, July 15th, 1940; not republished, but quoted by Weber, op. cit., p. 463n.
81. *Mémoires de guerre: L'Appel*, pp. 98-9.
82. ibid., p. 93.
83. There is the obvious anti-German caricature in the person of the school-teacher M. Rausch, with his hammer and his 'férocité naturelle', OC V, p. 247, and the more subtle references, analysed by 'Orion' (Jean Maze), the most interesting being the description of a character who spends two days in the priest's house as 'le zouave pontifical', ibid., p. 320: this, it seems, was the Resistance pseudonym of a secret agent who was hidden for a similar time by a real-life priest. Maze calls the allusion '(un) hommage plein de tact à l'action patriotique du clergé'; *Nouveau dictionnaire des girouettes*, Éditions le Régent, 1948, p. 51.
84. Preface to *Sainte Marguerite de Cortone*, OC VIII, p. 337.
85. 'La Foi en l'homme', *Gazette de Lausanne*, May 25th, 1943; J Occ, OC XI, pp. 352-4.
86. 'En marge d'une plaidoirie pour Jean-Jacques', J Occ, OC XI, pp. 324-6.
87. *La Résistance intellectuelle*, p. 76.
88. *Le Cahier noir*, OC XI, p. 367.

89. ibid., pp. 362-3.
90. ibid., p. 364.
91. OC XI, p. 376.
92. J I, OC XI, p. 47.
93. 'Vers un socialisme humaniste', *Le Figaro*, October 11th, 1944; BD, OC XI, p. 418.
94. 'Le Camp de la mort lente', *Le Figaro*, January 10th, 1945; BD, OC XI, pp. 476-8.
95. 'J. Prévost mort en combattant', *Le Figaro*, September 15th, 1944; BD, OC XI, pp. 405-7.
96. 'L'Événement est maître', *Le Figaro*, January 16th, 1945; BD, OC XI, pp. 480-1.
97. 'La Restauration de l'État', *Le Figaro*, November 3rd, 1944; BD, OC XI, p. 434.
98. 'Les Yeux des morts', *Le Figaro*, September 1st, 1944; BD, OC XI, p. 395.
99. 'Servir la France ressuscitée'. *Carrefour*, August 28th, 1944; BD, OC XI, p. 392.
100. 'Le Premier des nôtres', *Le Figaro*, August 25th, 1944; BD, OC XI, p. 391.
101. BD, OC XI, p. 393.
102. 'L'Avenir de la bourgeoisie', *Le Figaro*, October 3rd, 1944; BD, OC XI, p. 413.
103. ibid., p. 414.
104. 'La Vraie justice', *Le Figaro*, September 8th, 1944; BD, OC XI, p. 399.
105. 'Les Irréductibles', *Le Figaro*, September 6th, 1944; BD, OC XI, pp. 396-8.
106. 'Révolution et révolution', *Le Figaro*, October 13th, 1944; BD, OC XI, p. 420.
107. 'L'Inquiétude catholique en France', *Le Figaro*, November 1st, 1944; BD, OC XI, p. 431.
108. 'La Partie de belote', *Le Figaro*, March 1st, 1944; BD, OC XI, p. 497.
109. C. Mauriac, *Un autre de Gaulle*, Hachette, 1970, p. 95 (henceforth Claude Mauriac II).
110. De Gaulle, *Mémoires de guerre: L'Unité*, 187.
111. Claude Mauriac II, p. 61.
112. *De Gaulle*, p. 16.
113. Claude Mauriac II, pp. 95-6.
114. R.-L. Bruckberger, *Nous n'irons plus aux bois*, Amiot-Dumont, 1948, p. 33.
115. Claude Mauriac II, p. 83.
116. ibid., p. 49.
117. ibid., p. 83.
118. ibid., p. 62.
119. ibid., pp. 61-2.
120. Crozier, *De Gaulle, I: the warrior*, p. 315.
121. OC XI, preface, p. ii.
122. BD, OC XI, pp. 398-9.
123. BD, OC XI, pp. 419-21.
124. 'Justice', *Le Figaro*, December 12th, 1944; BD, OC XI, pp. 455-7.
125. 'Les conséquences politiques de l'épuration', *Le Figaro*, January 1st, 1945; BD, OC XI, p. 480. (Also MP, pp. 179-80.)
126. 'La Loterie', *Le Figaro*, December 27th, 1944; BD, OC XI, pp. 468-9.
127. BD, OC XI, pp. 455-7.
128. BD, OC XI, pp. 480-1.
129. 'En commençant par nous-mêmes', *Le Figaro*, February 23rd, 1945; BD, OC XI, pp. 494-5.
130. BD, OC XI, p. 479.

131. Claude Mauriac II, p. 95.
132. Vandromme, op. cit., p. 67.
133. R. Havard de la Montagne, *Histoire de l'Action Française*, Amiot-Dumont, 1950, p. 162.
134. Vandromme, op. cit., p. 65.
135. 'Le Sort tomba', *Le Figaro*, September 4th, 1944; BD, OC XI, pp. 473-4. (Also MP, p. 153.)
136. Claude Mauriac II, p. 52.
137. 'Le Procès d'un seul homme', *Le Figaro*, July 26th, 1945; J IV, p. 113. (Also MP, pp. 188-190.)
138. 'Lorenzaccio', *Le Figaro*, August 5th, 1945; J IV, pp. 117-9. (Also MP, pp. 190-2.)
139. 'A mi-chemin de la trahison et du sacrifice', *Le Figaro*, August 16th, 1945; J IV, pp. 127-9.
140. 'Autour d'un verdict', *Le Figaro*, January 4th, 1945; BD, OC XI, pp. 473-4.
141. L. Guitard, *Lettre sans malice à François Mauriac*, Martineau, 1967, pp. 24-7.
142. Bardèche, op. cit., pp. 57-8.
143. De Gaulle: *Mémoires de guerre: Le Salut*, Plon, 1959; Livre de poche edition, p. 136.
144. This and following information, Claude Mauriac II, pp. 59, 86.
145. Guitard, op. cit., p. 262.
146. R. Aron, *Histoire de l'épuration*, vol. II, Fayard, 1959, p. 349.
147. Claude Mauriac II, pp. 96-7.
148. MP, preface, p. 24.
149. 'L'Année de la réconciliation', *Le Figaro*, January 2nd, 1945; BD, OC XI, p. 471.
150. Claude Mauriac II, p. 93.
151. BD, OC XI, p. 472.
152. This paragraph is based on articles in *Le Bâillon dénoué*, OC XI, pp. 389-92 ('Le Premier des nôtres'), pp. 403-5 ('La Fortune de la France', *Le Figaro*, September 14th, 1944), pp. 433-5 ('La Restauration de l'État', *Le Figaro*, November 3rd, 1944), etc.
153. Claude Mauriac II, p. 80.
154. *Mémoires de guerre: L'Unité*, pp. 221-2.
155. *Mémoires de guerre: Le Salut*, p. 112.
156. This and following information from Claude Mauriac II, pp. 98-9.
157. ibid., p. 81.
158. ibid., pp. 170, 206.
159. 'Un discours de M. Léon Blum', *Le Figaro*, May 24th, 1945; J IV, p. 64.
160. 'L'Anniversaire', *Le Figaro*, June 19th, 1945; J IV, p. 85.
161. 'Le Débat sur la constituante', *Le Figaro*, June 28th, 1945; J IV, pp. 90-1.
162. 'Le Gouvernement et les partis', *Le Figaro*, September 12th, 1945; J IV, p. 137.
163. 'Le Champ clos', *Le Figaro*, November 18th, 1945; MP, pp. 239-40.
164. J IV, p. 225-5. (Also MP, pp. 244-6.)
165. Claude Mauriac II, p. 168.
166. ibid., p. 203.
167. *Le Figaro*, October 1st, 1946.
168. Claude Mauriac II, pp. 239-40.
169. 'Bon an, mal an', *Le Figaro*, January 1st, 1947; J V, pp. 134-5.
170. Claude Mauriac II, p. 271.

171. Crozier: *De Gaulle, II: The Statesman*, 1973, p. 416.

172. 'Réponse à Albert Camus', *La Table ronde*, February 1949; MP, p. 274.

173. *De Gaulle*, p. 56.

174. *Nouveaux mémoires intérieurs*, p. 243.

175. *De Gaulle*, p. 56.

176. MP, p. 274.

177. 'Les Baudruches crevées', *La Table ronde*, May 1951; MP, pp. 287-8.

178. M. Schumann, *Le Vrai malaise des intellectuels de gauche*, Plon, 1957, p. 17.

179. 'La Tentation de l'écrivain', *Le Figaro*, September 29th, 1944; BD, OC XI, pp. 411-2.

180. 'Une immense espérance', *Le Figaro*, January 26th, 1945; J IV, p. 12-13.

181. 'L'Épouvantail', *Le Figaro*, July 17th, 1945; J IV, pp. 103-4.

182. 'Le Fait communiste', *Le Figaro*, November 22nd, 1945; J IV, p. 181.

183. 'Le Masque à la main', *Le Figaro*, January 1st, 1946; J IV, pp. 210-11, (also MP, pp. 337-8). See also Mauriac's preface to B. Just, *Un procès préfabriqué*, Editions du Témoignage chrétien, 1949.

184. 'Socialistes et communistes', *Le Figaro*, January 13th, 1946; J IV, p. 219.

185. 'Le Malentendu', *Le Figaro*, July 19th, 1946; J V, p. 63.

186. 'Les Deux églises', *Le Figaro*, September 12th, 1946; J V, p. 103.

187. 'Le Crime des innocents', *Le Figaro*, October 24th, 1949; MP, p. 384.

188. 'Le Pauvre intellectuel communiste', *Le Figaro*, May 22nd, 1950; MP, p. 395.

189. 'Défense des bien-pensants', *Le Figaro*, February 21st, 1946; J IV, p. 229.

190. 'Le Point de rencontre', *Le Figaro*, March 28th, 1947; J V, p. 162.

191. *Terres franciscaines*, Plon, 1950, p. 14.

192. *La Pierre d'achoppement*, p. 69.

193. BN I, p. 244.

194. 'La Guerre aux catholiques', *Le Figaro*, December 16th, 1945; J IV, pp. 202-3. (Also MP, pp. 329-31.)
     'La Seule question', *Le Figaro*, December 19th, 1945; J IV, p. 204, (Also MP, pp. 331-2.)
     'Paroles de paix', *Le Figaro*, December 23rd, 1945; J IV, pp. 207-8. (Also MP, pp. 333-5.)
     'La Parole de la France', *Le Figaro*, March 14th, 1949; MP, p. 378. *etc.*

195. See above, p. 90.

196. 'L'Orage sous la coupole', *Le Figaro*, September 21st, 1944; J IV, pp. 5-7.

197. BN I, p. 206.

198. 'Les Origines d'un mouvement', *Le Figaro*, October 3rd, 1945; J IV, pp. 151-2.

199. 'Cléricalisme', *Le Figaro*, October 28th-29th, 1945; J IV, pp. 159-60.

200. 'L'Autre danger', *Le Figaro*, March 19th, 1946; J V, p. 15.

201. *Nouveaux mémoires intérieurs*, p. 243.

202. 'L'Absurde', *Le Figaro*, April 23rd, 1946; J V, p. 40. (Also MP, p. 248.)

203. J V, pp. 135-6.

204. 'Remonter à la source', *Le Figaro*, October 22nd, 1947; J V, pp. 228-30.

205. 'Écrit le premier janvier 1944', *Almanach des Lettres Françaises*, 1944; MP, p. 139.

206. 'La Faillite' and 'Encore le bonheur', *Le Figaro*, December 13th, 1945, and September 20th, 1946, respectively; J IV, pp. 199-201 and J V, p. 108.

207. 'Bloc occidental? Non: Europe', *Le Figaro*, September 15th, 1945; J IV, p. 138. (Also MP, p. 227.)

208. *La Nation Française a une âme*, OC XI, pp. 370-1. (Also MP, pp. 157-8).
209. 'La Nouvelle alliance', *Le Figaro*, December 14th, 1944; BD, OC XI, pp. 457-8.
210. 'L'Anniversaire', *Le Figaro*, June 19th, 1945; J IV, p. 85.
211. 'Le Parti du refus', *Le Figaro*, July 20th-21st, 1947; J V, p. 198.
212. 'Propos d'un cannibale', *Le Figaro*, October 10th, 1950; MP, p. 403.
213. BN I, pp. 108, 189, 270-2.
214. 'Après la conférence de presse', *Le Figaro*, June 5th, 1945; J IV, p. 74.
215. 'Plainte', *Le Figaro*, October 5th, 1944; BD, OC XI, p. 415.
216. 'La Raisonnable entente', *Le Figaro*, June 21st, 1945; J IV, pp. 85-7.
217. BN II, p. 242.
218. BN II, p. 391.
219. 'La Machine infernale', *Le Figaro*, July 4th, 1947; J V, pp. 192-3. The article bearing this title in MP, pp. 363-5, and dated July 1947, is not the same article and appears to have been included in error.
220. 'Le Monolithe et le roseau', *Le Figaro*, June 13th, 1948; MP, pp. 265-6.
221. 'Réponse à Albert Camus', *La Table ronde*, February 1949; MP, p. 274.
222. 'La Petite fille', *Le Figaro*, March 23rd, 1945; J IV, p. 28.
223. 'Saturne', *Le Figaro*, September 5th, 1947; MP, p. 367.
224. 'Les Droits de l'homme', *Le Figaro*, February 21st, 1945; BD, OC XI, pp. 493-4. 'L'Enjeu', *Le Figaro*, September 18th, 1945; J IV, p. 143.
225. e.g. 'Pour éviter le pire', *Le Figaro*, January 5th, 1954; MP, pp. 317-18.
226. 'Ici et maintenant', *Le Figaro*, May 3rd, 1947; MP, p. 256.
227. Vandromme, op. cit., p. 63.
228. MP, preface, p. 26.
229. See the articles of January 28th, 1953, in *La Vigie marocaine* and *Le Petit marocain*, as well as *Paris-Match*, February 7th, 1953.
230. Preface to R. Barrat, op. cit., Seuil, 1953, p. 13.
231. BN I, p. 118.
232. BN I, p. 88.
233. BN I, p. 69.
234. BN I, p. 55.
235. BN I, p. 67.
236. BN I, p. 85.
237. BN I, pp. 189, 269.
238. BN I, p. 53.
239. BN II, p. 31.
240. BN I, pp. 211, 262, 303; BN II, p. 46, etc.
241. BN I, p. 283.
242. BN II, pp. 23-4.
243. BN I, p. 121.
244. 'L'Homme malade', *Le Figaro*, June 3rd, 1953; MP, p. 308.
245. BN I, p. 111.
246. BN I, p. 193.
247. A, Werth, *The Strange history of Pierre Mendès-France*, Barrie, 1957, p. 79.

CHAPTER FOUR

1. 'L'Épreuve des faits', *Le Figaro*, January 23rd, 1947; MP, pp. 253-5.
2. 'Le Dernier rempart', *Le Figaro*, July 24th, 1948; MP, pp. 267-8.
3. BN I, p. 57.
4. Claude Mauriac II, p. 394.
5. BN I, pp. 72-3.
6. BN I, pp. 158-9.
7. BN I, p. 235.
8. BN I, p. 267.
9. BN I, p. 284.
10. BN I, p. 288.
11. BN I, p. 368.
12. BN II, p. 55.
13. BN II, p. 57.
14. BN II, p. 66.
15. BN II, p. 75.
16. BN II, p. 100.
17. BN II, p. 107.
18. BN II, pp. 109-10.
19. BN V, p. 323.
20. BN III, pp. 125, 155, etc.
21. BN II, p. 333.
22. BN III, pp. 8-9.
23. BN III, p. 288.
24. BN III, p. 378.
25. BN II, p. 200.
26. BN II, p. 307.
27. BN II, p. 373.
28. BN II, p. 352.
29. BN II, p. 112.
30. BN II, p. 203.
31. BN II, p. 188.
32. BN III, pp. 132-3.
33. BN II, p. 258.
34. BN III, p. 146.
35. BN III, p. 119.
36. BN IV, p. 347.
37. BN IV, p. 65.
38. BN II, pp. 238, 242.
39. BN III, p. 236.
40. BN IV, p. 58.
41. BN II, p. 251.
42. BN III, p. 192.
43. BN III, p. 20.
44. BN III, p. 262.
45. BN III, p. 162.
46. BN III, p. 31.
47. BN III, p. 38.
48. BN III, p. 266.
49. BN III, p. 342.
50. BN III, p. 146.
51. BN III, p. 223.
52. BN III, p. 106 (my italics).
53. BN II, p. 68.
54. BN II, p. 206.
55. BN III, p. 39.
56. BN III, p. 185.
57. BN IV, p. 12.
58. BN III, p. 442.
59. BN IV, p. 316, etc.
60. BN V, pp. 38-9.
61. BN III, pp. 121-2.
62. BN III, p. 161.
63. BN III, p. 146.
64. BN III, p. 193.
65. BN III, p. 414.
66. BN III, p. 8.
67. BN III, p. 414.
68. BN III, p. 324.
69. BN III, pp. 279-80.
70. BN III, p. 231.
71. BN III, p. 6.
72. BN III, p. 373.
73. ibid.
74. BN III, p. 439.
75. BN IV, p. 51.
76. J. Mauriac, *Mort du général de Gaulle*, Grasset, 1972, p. 135.
77. BN IV, p. 243.
78. BN IV, p. 26.
79. ibid.
80. BN IV, p. 430.
81. BN III, p. 18.
82. BN IV, pp. 138, 155.
83. BN V, pp. 58-9.
84. BN V, p. 60. See also A. Hartley, *Gaullism*, Routledge & Kegan Paul, 1972, p. 279.

85. BN V, p. 63.
86. BN V, pp. 71-2.
87. BN V, pp. 60-1, 128.
88. BN V, pp. 79.
89. BN V, p. 171.
90. BN V, p. 172.
91. BN V, p. 83.
92. BN IV, p. 261.
93. BN V, p. 70.
94. BN V, p. 78.
95. BN V, p. 66.
96. BN V, pp. 87, 207-8, etc.
97. BN V, pp. 169-70.
98. BN V, p. 67.
99. BN V, p. 129.
100. BN V, p. 68.
101. BN V, pp. 81-2.
102. BN III, p. 258.
103. BN V, pp. 60, 78-9, 80, 177, etc.
104. BN V, p. 328.

CHAPTER FIVE

1. Vandromme, op. cit., pp. 85-6.
2. Grall, op. cit., pp. 77-8.
3. See Mauriac: 'A une dame qui voulait m'envoyer le Dictionnaire des girouettes', *La Table ronde*, April 1950; MP, pp. 278-81. Maze: 'François Mauriac inventeur', *Écrits de Paris*, June 1950; Nocher, op. cit., *passim*. Schumann, op. cit., pp. 7-14.
4. *Lettres ouvertes*, p. 55. Also BN II, p. 69.
5. OC XI, preface, p. ii.
6. BD, OC XI, p. 418.
7. *Le Cahier noir*, OC XI, p. 362.
8. BN I, p. 320.
9. 'L'Épreuve de silence', *La Gazette de Lausanne*, October 9th, 1942; J Occ, OC XI, p. 336.
10. *Mémoires intérieurs*, pp. 129-31.
11. 'Un certain regard', *Le Figaro*, August 4th, 1937; J III, p. 210.
12. J Occ, OC XI, p. 352.
13. 'Le Conflit spirituel', *Le Figaro*, May 10th, 1945; J IV, p. 58.
14. 'Oui plutôt deux fois qu'une', *Le Figaro*, October 16th, 1945; MP, p. 231.
15. BN I, p. 331.
16. *Ce que je crois*, pp. 115-16.
17. J V, p. 139.
18. 'Le Combat des deux cités', *Le Figaro*, October 11th, 1947; J V, p. 223.
19. BN III, p. 260.
20. *Le Cahier noir*, OC XI, p. 362; MP, p. 131.
21. ibid., OC XI, p. 367, MP, p. 137.
22. *Le Fils de l'homme*, Grasset, 1958, p. 20.
23. 'Un dernier mot', *Le Figaro*, August 19th, 1945; J IV, p. 130.
24. 'La Bombe', *Le Figaro*, August 10th, 1945; J IV, p. 123.
25. BN II, p. 397.
26. MP, p. 271.
27. 'Premier jour de vacances', *Le Figaro*, July 25th, 1947; J V, p. 201.
28. 'La Mère humiliée', *Nineteenth Century and After*, London, October 1940; J Occ, OC XI, p. 314. (Also MP, p. 128.)

29. 'Le Pharisien malgré lui', *Le Temps présent*, December 15th, 1939; MP, p. 119.

30. BN I, pp. 309-10.

31. MP, p. 139.

32. 'Pour le peuple basque', *Le Figaro*, June 17th, 1937; MP, p. 82.

33. MP, p. 271.

34. *Les Voix intérieures*, quoted in 'La Lecture du milieu de la nuit', *Le Figaro*, August 23rd, 1946; J V, p. 90.

35. BN I, p. 96.

36. 'L'Homme inhumain', *Le Figaro*, May 12th-13th, 1946; J V, p. 49.

37. BN II, p. 206.

38. BN II, p. 295.

39. BN II, p. 373.

40. 'Un peuple irresponsable de son histoire', *Le Figaro*, April 8th, 1952; MP, p. 294.

41. BN II, p. 193.

42. MP, p. 275.

43. *Les Déracinés*, *L'Œuvre de Maurice Barrès*, vol. 3, p. 195.

44. ibid., p. 179.

45. De Gaulle, *Mémoires d'Espoir*, vol. I, Plon, 1970; Livre de Poche edition, p. 39.

46. BN V, p. 218.

47. BN III, p. 187.

48. BN III, p. 266.

49. BN V, p. 73.

50. *Mémoires de guerre: L'Appel*, p. 6.

51. *Mémoires de guerre: Le Salut*, p. 110.

52. *Le Fil de l'épée*, Éditions Berger-Levrault, 1944; 10/18 edition (Union générale d'éditions), p. 10.

53. ibid., p. 73-6.

54. See above, p. 29.

55. *Le Fil de l'épée*, p. 7.

56. ibid., pp. 22-3.

57. BN III, p. 266.

58. 'La Diversité francaise', *Le Figaro*, November 28th, 1944; BD, OC XI, p. 446.

59. *Mémoires de guerre: L'Unité*, p. 379.

60. ibid., p. 378.

61. *Les Déracinés*, *L'Œuvre de Maurice Barrès*, vol. 3, pp. 343-4.

62. J.-M. Domenach, *Barrès par lui-même*, Éditions du Seuil, 1962, p. 54.

63. *Les Déracinés*, *L'Appel au soldat*, *L'Œuvre de Maurice Barrès*, vol. 3, p. 24, vol. 4, pp. 62-3, respectively.

64. See *Les Déracinés*, loc. cit., p. 209.

65. *L'Appel au soldat*, loc. cit., vol. 3, pp. 461-2.

66. BN III, p. 133.

67. *Les Déracinés*, loc. cit., p. 210.

68. Bainville, op. cit., p. 69.

69. BN II, p. 135.